Young, Woke and Christian:
Words from a Missing Generation

Young, Woke and Christian

Words from a Missing Generation

Edited by
Victoria Turner

scm press

Published in 2022 by SCM Press
Editorial office
3rd Floor, Invicta House,
108–114 Golden Lane,
London EC1Y 0TG, UK
www.scmpress.co.uk

SCM Press is an imprint of Hymns Ancient & Modern Ltd
(a registered charity)

Hymns Ancient & Modern® is a registered trademark of
Hymns Ancient & Modern Ltd
13A Hellesdon Park Road, Norwich,
Norfolk NR6 5DR, UK

British Library Cataloguing in Publication data
A catalogue record for this book is available
from the British Library

ISBN 978-0-334-06153-3

Typeset by Regent Typesetting
Printed and bound by
CPI Group (UK) Ltd

Contents

Acknowledgements

The first person who deserves acknowledgement for this project is Anthony Reddie. He is a friend, mentor, advisor and inspiration for many, and for me this usually comes in the form of an angry push towards confidence. Thank you for your belief in this project right from the beginning. I also need to acknowledge Michael Jagessar, whose 'thinking outside the box-ness' and daring radicalness has helped shaped my own approach to theology, overcome imposter syndrome and throw myself into my intimidating ideas. Many incredible academics, teachers and ministers have read drafts and contributed to these chapters, namely Eve Parker, Ulrich Schmiedel, Jarel Robinson-Brown, Hannah Brown, Kayla Robbins, Alex Clare-Young, John Swinton, Katie Cross, Llinos Mai, Ruth Harvey, Ed Davis and Chris Greenough. Em Lister, Ian Rowe and Guillermo Diaz de Liaño del Valle have been constantly supportive throughout this project – thank you! Finally, thank you Liz, Nosa, Kirsty, Chrissie, Josh, Jack, Annie, Shermara, Anna, Molly, Annika, Sophie, Laura and Sam for seeing the vision and plunging into your writing with enthusiasm and energy.

Prologue

ANTHONY REDDIE

Young, Woke and Christian: Words from a Missing Generation is a remarkable and hugely important book and I am delighted, dare I say honoured, to be asked to write the Prologue.

As an experienced Black theologian who has been researching and writing for almost 25 years, I have long learnt about and come to understand the various significant categories that shape the undertaking of liberation theology. All forms of liberation theology have as their point of departure the lived realities of human struggle and marginalization. The group identity, or what is sometimes called 'identity politics', in which human beings seek solidarity with like-minded individuals who share their experience and condition, is the basic platform on which various forms of liberation theologies are based. There would be no viable movement of any form of liberation theology if there were no sense of shared experience among those who are socially marginalized for a whole variety of reasons.

Women fighting patriarchy, sexism and other forms of male privilege. Black people fighting White supremacy and racism. Poor people fighting neo-liberalism and capitalism. LGBTQ+ people fighting the toxic dangers of heteronormativity and gender binaries. Or disabled people fighting the oppressive restrictions of so-called 'able-bodied' frameworks of normality. In each context, the basis of all liberation theologies remains the theo-praxis of seeking to bring about revolutionary change. In one sense *Young, Woke and Christian: Words from a Missing Generation* is 'simply' an important compendium of liberationist writings from an impressive younger generation of theologians and activists.

In that guise, this remains an importantly vibrant and no-holds-barred text calling for the forms of liberation-inspired discipleship that should be second nature to the Church, but which all too often have proved elusive. The chapters in this book address the various categories of the social practice of exclusion that have marginalized and oppressed millions of people across the world. So we have chapters exploring the impact of racism on Black bodies, sexism and patriarchy on women, poverty and homelessness on those marginalized from 'mainstream' society, rigid gender binaries on trans people, heteronormativity on gay and lesbian communities, the fixities of alleged mental health norms for those struggling with mental health challenges, and those who are disabled, wrestling with the constructions of societies created with able-bodied people in mind.

These chapters in themselves are a bold restatement of the need for a form of Christianity that responds to the radicality of being 'woke'. Being a man in his mid-50s, 'being woke' is not a term to which I naturally gravitate. Woke is for the young. In my youth we spoke of people being 'conscious'. Back in the middle to late 1980s, I co-created a short-lived Black activist group called 'Conscious Nubians', in which we called for a form of Black radicalism that challenged the Church to harness the emotive power of Black youth. The Church did not heed our voices and the group soon dissipated.

Fast track from the moribund world of Thatcherism, gross materialism and the conservative restrictions of British churches of the late 1980s to 2021 and the radical joy of this book. A book that is commendably diverse and inclusive, seeking to model the very qualities of the gospel of Jesus Christ and the traditions of radicalism and liberative praxis that should be the norm for the Church. It says a great deal about the culture wars in which we are presently immersed that *woke* has become a term of abuse from some, as if the opposite of woke is something neutral or even respectable. Let's be clear, to be anti-woke is to be pro-White supremacy, neo-colonialist, misogynistic and bound to a status quo posture that supports a world in which Covid-19 could prey on the poor and flourish against a backdrop of the systemic racism that murdered George Floyd and countless others.

And yet, while lauding the book for the ways in which it celebrates a younger generation of activist theologians, I want to suggest that it is doing something much more radical than first appears to be the case. Namely, that *Young, Woke and Christian: Words from a Missing Generation* is proffering a new category for liberation theology, one that I will term 'being young'. Suggesting that being young is a category of marginalization in itself is not without its problems. Not all young adults and people are marginalized. Not all young people are woke or conscious or committed to liberative praxis. I want to suggest that being young is a category in itself because of how they have traditionally been treated by the Church and wider society. My initial thinking against this notion lay in the fact that being young is not a permanent category, i.e. most young people grow older (I have resisted the term 'grow up'). I was once the age of these writers of this very fine book.

Further reflection, however, made me revise my reaction to this initial thought. Poverty is not necessarily permanent for all people, but we count it as a major category in liberation theology. The rise in trans rights has reminded us of the illusion of the permanency of gender binaries. So the fact that people will grow through the biological chronology of time and human maturation should not be a reason for not seeing the condition of being young as a form of marginalization in itself, given the ways in which churches continue to patronize, fetishize and simply ignore young people.

I remember preaching a sermon in the chapel at Regent's Park College (Oxford University) in the Michaelmas term of 2020. This service in Advent focused on Mary, the mother of Jesus, a teenage girl speaking prophetically as detailed in the Magnificat. In preparation for delivering the sermon, I undertook research looking at two iconic young women, Malala

Yousafzai and Greta Thunberg. Looking at social media linked to both figures, I found a great deal of negative reaction to them, a good deal of it aimed at their youth and their presumption in lecturing older people on how we should behave as humans. The criticisms were also a product of their gender, in which predominantly middle-aged, cisgender men felt it appropriate to ridicule these two young women. In my subsequent sermon, I argued that Malala Yousafzai and Greta Thunberg were prophets in our midst. The fact that they were young and women was precisely what made their respective activism so very prophetic.

It is no accident that the thrust for a radical response to climate change is coming from the young. Similarly, the thrust for trans rights and White allyship has also come from the young. *Young, Woke and Christian: Words from a Missing Generation* offers a bold and prophetic vision for a radical liberationist mode of Christian faith that speaks to the need for churches to become allies to all those who are marginalized and oppressed. It is a bold call for Christianity to rediscover its radical roots and to side with the powerless, the weak, the poor, the broken-hearted and those who are told that they do not count and that their lives do not matter. This task is one of righteousness and salvation. In our present age, for this generation, we are using the term 'woke'. Whether we call it woke, or consciousness as in my day, or even more traditionally, righteousness, the call to move beyond bland neutrality or, even worse, actively colluding with empire, greed and the status quo of vested interests is one that remains the rock centre of this fine and excellent book. I am honoured to be associated with it.

Professor Anthony Reddie
Regent's Park College, University of Oxford
and the University of South Africa

When Black Goes Breathless

Samuel Nwokoro, Edinburgh, May 2020
In memory of George Floyd

I thought I was strong
I believed they would never break me
That their hate will never pay
Until one more life pleaded

I thought the human breath was sacred
A mark of equality and dignity
That everyone breathes and deserves to
Until one more breath was suffocated

I thought they were here to protect
I believed it was their mandate
That lives are safe with them around
Until one more life was taken

I thought the human body to be all the same
I believed Melanin was just a chemical
That it would never matter that much
Until another black skin bled

I thought that the neck was fragile
I believed that only the last resort aimed for it
That only violent criminals go neck first
Until one more neck cracked

I thought when people bow the knee
Someone is about to pray, help, or propose
That only such noble purposes are worthy
Until one bent in murder of the helpless

I thought being black was beautiful
Debunking the premise of the Cornerstone
Giving the world the best of itself
Until his crime was being black

I thought that only children call out for their mum
That 'Mama!' was their sweet *caprice*
Making attention or grief known
Until I heard a grown man cry 'Mama!'

I thought people are innocent until proven guilty
I believed arrest to bear no verdict
That it is just the beginning
Until he was tried and condemned by the sidewalk

I can only hope that George would be the last
The last neck to feel the weight of an angry knee
The last reason for cities to burn
The last black to go breathless!

Introduction: 'Coming Out as Christian'

VICTORIA TURNER

The idea for this book stemmed from a thought during a typical lockdown lunch. After reading another tweet about how young people are not concerned with the Church, I turned to my partner and said, 'I think my dream is just to write a book called "Young, Woke and Christian" that just explains to the bemused older generations that there are young people in the Church who do care about Jesus, alongside caring about politics and justice – and that they care about politics and justice and all this "snowflake" stuff because they love Jesus.'

'Okay, do it,' he replied in his usual direct, Spanish style. 'What, no, I can't do that, I have to do a PhD, I can't write a book!' And I was right, I could not have written this book. Part of the reasoning for this labour of love is that there is a lot of literature 'about' young people in the Church, trying to understand them, categorize them, mission towards them, evangelize them and entice them with capitalistic tools and schemes. If I were to write another book 'about' young people, even with my own identity as a young person, I would just be adding to the pile. As an edited book, however, I am able to elevate incredible young people, who have written differently (and sometimes better than me), who come from varied backgrounds and who are passionate about the same topics as I am – and more. Reading over their chapters has brought me joy, sadness and frustration (at the themes, never their writing!), but overwhelmingly, hope. I feel we have been able to articulate what it means to have faith as a young person today, and also explain how sometimes having that faith within the existing institutional structures of the Church brings us difficulties and tension.

This book is an attempt to relay the experience(s) of being the younger generation in British Church today. Although we have ecumenical representation, the chapter contributors identify with either the Church of England, the United Reformed Church, the Baptist Union, or the Methodist Church, namely only the 'historic denominations', apart from Shermara who has roots in the Pentecostal tradition. Additionally, we are all privileged to be in some kind of leadership role in, or connected to, our churches. This factor helped me choose each contributor, believing that their gifts were obvious and powerful, but it also limits the scope of this book. There are so many other young people in churches whose gifts are often unacknowledged. This collection of young people is also very female heavy. This was not conscious on my part, but I am not particularly saddened by it (how exciting for a book not about women to be dominated by women!). There are also issues/ chapters I would have liked to include, but my own interest in Palestinian liberation, World Christianity, empire, colonialism and mission, capitalism and global economic injustices are themes that could not be included due to space. The topics discussed are those relevant to the British Church. Perhaps we could have a *Young, Woke and Christian* Vol. II at some point that digs deeper beyond our own context.[1] I hope the passion of these chosen chapters incites conversations in all levels of the Church today, and not only changes how we perceive the roles of young people in our church structures and institutions, but also how we understand the very role of those church institutions.

Contentious titling: thinking about wokeness

> The call to dethrone white supremacy and patriarchy within the Church is not an issue of political correctness nor is it merely an appeal to 'wokeness'. It is a gospel issue.[2]

I could not agree more with Chine McDonald's claim. The word 'woke' first seriously entered my agenda after reading Lauren Duca's *How to Start a Revolution: Young People and the Future of Politics*. Duca, exploring the political awakening among young people after the 2016 election of Trump, explains,

> The idea of wokeness entered the conversation as a way of understanding tragedy in the context of systemic racism. Being 'woke' is about processing atrocities through the system that allows them to routinely occur ... Strong political opinions became a social necessity.[3]

In the UK context, I propose that it was Jeremy Corbyn's run up to the 2017 and 2019 elections against Theresa May and Boris Johnson that sparked a similar 'political awakening'.[4] A study by YouGov revealed that age was the biggest dividing line in British politics in the EU Referendum and the 2017 and 2019 elections, with the statistic that 'every 10 years older a voter is, their chance of voting Tory increases by around nine points, and the chance of them voting Labour decreases by eight points'.[5] I remember feeling an energy at Corbyn's address on Bristol's College Green in 2019 that could only be compared to a large charismatic worship gathering. The majority of the audience were young people, students. By contrast, on the night of his defeat, my social media feeds were filled with my friends crying. We had tried so hard, been more invested in politics than ever before, we'd had numerous arguments with lazy friends who were bewildered and did not feel informed enough to vote, we broke friendships with those backing the righter-than-right-wing Tory government. We saw how the media vilified our aubergine-growing, justice-orientated, lovable grandad hero. His defeat felt like a betrayal from the older generations, who had already ruined many prospects with Brexit, and now blocked the path towards fixing some of them.[6] After the 2019 election there was certainly a slump and a feeling of disbelief that I still struggle with now, especially any time I open my Twitter feed. The injustices that caused the Black Lives Matter protests and have surrounded the Covid-19 pandemic, however, have made the spark of awakening erupt into a fire of consciousness. The government's response to Covid-19 in the UK has created a similar 'social necessity' in Britain that is described by Duca. An obvious example, reflected on by Anna in Chapter 9, involved children and school meals. Not only had our Prime Minister exploited our vulnerable, the 'necessary sacrifices' for his precious economy, but now his government was happily exploiting the poor for profit.[7] Circumstances such as these have woken up our generation to the injustices in our political structures and capitalistic climate.

Duca, however, does not clearly distinguish between her use of 'awakening' and her occasional use of 'woke', tending to only use 'woke' when referring to events such as Black Lives Matter. This is because Duca is a white person, and I am a white person, and that means our experiences of what it means to be and feel 'woke' are very different to a black person's experience of 'wokeness'. The phrase 'stay woke' was a popular slogan during the Black Lives Matter protests in 2014 after the death of Michael Brown in Missouri, and resurfaced more recently after the death of George Floyd on May 26, 2020. Romano, who traced the history of the term for a popular article, writes that linguistically 'woke' connects with the black consciousness movement in the early twentieth century, especially with the Jamaican philosopher Marcus Garvey's 1923 summons 'Wake Up Ethiopia! Wake up Africa!'[8] Romano continues,

A few years later, the phrase 'stay woke' turned up as part of a spoken afterword in the 1938 song 'Scottsboro Boys', a protest song by Blues musician Huddie Ledbetter, a.k.a. Lead Belly. The song describes the 1931 saga of a group of nine Black teenagers in Scottsboro, Arkansas, who were accused of raping two white women ... Lead Belly uses 'stay woke' in explicit association with Black Americans' need to be aware of racially motivated threats and the potential dangers of white America.[9]

There are hints of the idea of wokeness in the First National Conference of Colored Women in Boston in 1895. Fannie Barrier Williams, who had been banned from the racist white women's club that was working towards giving women the vote (after a legacy of abolitionist activism), exclaimed that

> progress means a great deal more than what is generally meant by the terms culture, education and contact ... The [black women's] club movement is well purposed ... It is rather the force of a new intelligence against the old ignorance. The struggle of an enlightened consciousness against the whole brood of social miseries, born out of the stress and pain of a hated past.[10]

Williams hints at the idea of a woke worldview with the idea of a 'new intelligence' and 'enlightened consciousness' that can only be developed from the plethora of struggles black women face and is directed against the unjust normality of society. Theologically, the concept of black consciousness, as connected by Anthony Reddie in the prologue, was already strongly outlined by Professor Allan Boesak in 1976, in the early days of his struggle for liberation from South African Apartheid. Boesak connected the concepts of Black Power and Black Theology to overcome the oppressive mentality of less-than-whiteness that the White church in South Africa, through State theology, connected to Jesus and the chosen-ness of the white race. Black love, he wrote, is required for black people to see themselves in the salvation story and to contextualize the gospel in the light of their struggle to liberate themselves from religious, economic, psychological, and cultural dependency on White hierarchy and systems.[11]

The universal cry for black consciousness to 'stay woke' is not, therefore, one that involves white people. We, I, do not *need* to stay woke. We can choose to be woke. So why have I used this charged word for the title? Mostly I'm reacting to the mainstream antagonistic use of the word. Here are some Tweets I have come across since editing this book:

> The gospel is about salvation by faith in Jesus. In any case, saying that the gospel is about social justice is anachronistic. Awake. Wokeness, on the other hand, is all about divisive identity politics which is antithetical to the gospel.[12]

On a similar theme to this Tweet, there was a whole conference in Denton, Texas, named 'Wokeness and the Gospel' on the 11–12 June 2021, supported by evangelical churches and seminaries, that sought to stand against the false religion of wokeness and proclaim the truth of Jesus.[13]

Another set of anti-woke sentiments came from multiple replies after the #DismantlingWhiteness hashtag began trending from Oxford University Regents Park College's Critical White Theology conference. These included:

> The only racists en mass are the hard left the woke and #blm. They are trying to destroy society, they are bringing everyone down to their level.[14]

> The woke 'Christian' crazies who started #Dismantling-Whiteness are doing the usual tactic of now crying victim and accusing detractors of 'white fragility' … Keep up the criticism and we'll continue #DismantlingWokeness.[15]

This debate achieves nothing, other then [sic] give Blacks who are anti white and the woke brigade a stick to beat natives with.[16]

Do you woke leftist ****s even realize how disgusting and racist your own movement is? Take your communism elsewhere.[17]

The word woke was not used in the conference.[18] It was used by other white people, offended by the progressive agenda, to silence and dismiss the conference by arguing that 'wokeness' was racist towards white people. The language of 'natives' to describe white British people, and the phrase 'down to their level' to describe inclusivity tactics in solidarity with non-white people, display how the term woke is seen as a threat to the status quo of white, patriarchal, heteronormativity in British society.[19]

These, of course, are extreme examples from evangelical, conservative Christians and nationalistic white English people. I suggest, however, that young people are faced with frequently being silenced about their politics in the Church. On the 28 October 2020, the 'Ecumenical Council for Corporate Responsibility' hosted a conversation with Ruth Valerio and Rowan Williams along the theme of 'Restoring Hope'.[20] One of the questions from an audience member outlined,

Young people are passionate about social justice issues and the environment because it makes them feel better.

In churches, where we are very often the minority, young people's political agendas are often silenced with the label of 'woke'. Woke is the umbrella term used by those who want society to stay the same to describe progressive ideals that change the status quo of injustice in society. Instead of bringing connotations of the historic resistance of black victims to a structurally racist society (notwithstanding the intersectionality it also addresses), it has become a word that allows our activism to stay on the fringes of church life – as an added extra, something young people might grow out of, something the church can perhaps do on Wednesday afternoons rather than realizing that this 'wokeness' they are dismissing needs to be integrated into the whole church.

The multi-dimensional existence of the term woke has created a debate about who can possibly use the term authentically, without appropriating its history, meaning and agenda. I personally would take it as a compliment to be called woke, but I would not call myself woke. In a group discussion about this, the majority of the contributors to this book felt the same. The term 'woke' is not for us (the white contributors) to reclaim. It is a state of being, a resilience, that we cannot claim to share (because we do not need to stay woke in the face of racism); we can only admire the resilient wokeness of resistance from others – hopefully in solidarity. On the other hand, we see how, as a collective in a group of young people, our passions are dismissed as another agenda from the 'woke generation'. The themes dealt with in this book are perceived by our silencers as 'woke' issues, revolutionist ideas that perform a theoretical utopia rather than argue for real change. I recently heard a story of a local congregation not installing a disabled access ramp because they did not have any disabled members in the congregation. The theory of disability justice was seen as a distant, woke idea that had no relevance to the able-bodied members. Our ideology of justice at the heart of our congregations, that is labelled as woke, looks to re-centre at whatever cost those who are pushed to the sidelines. Those who it threatens to displace from all-encompassing power – usually those who are white, male, heterosexual, cisgender, able-bodied, middle-class – are often blind to the realities of bodies that are unlike their own and so do not see a need for change. My generation, which *is* active in the Church, is working to change that. This book aims to amplify their voices and argue that young people are not only *in* the Church already, but they are *changing* the Church already – a Church that desperately needs to change. Each individual chapter in this book, therefore, does not need to deal explicitly with the concept of 'woke', as it is not a term we would choose to describe ourselves and our work as Christians, activists, protestors, academics, church leaders, ecumenical leaders, deacons, mathematicians and scientists. 'Woke' is a term, however, that we are tired of battling against. Our work cannot be dismissed any longer, and the appropriation of such a rich term likewise needs to cease.

Coming Out as Christian

I was on a train to Oban, to visit Iona with a friend who was brought up a Muslim and now studies for a PhD in Edinburgh. When describing why I believe we need this book she exclaimed, 'It sounds like coming out.' 'Yes! Coming out as Christian,' I replied.

Being heterosexual I have not had to 'come out' myself, so I was delighted when my bisexual friend made this link. This analogy is helpful for understanding how it feels to be a Christian in the public square of the UK today. The general perception of Christianity, when I talk to peers who are not Christian, is that we are evangelizing, Empire loving, gay hating, no sex demanding, buzz-kills/party-poopers. This is obviously a silly over-simplification, but I find when I meet somebody in Britain – especially someone around my age – who does not share the experience of having faith, I spend so much time explaining the type of Christian that I am *not*, that there is no space to share the joy I receive from being the type of Christian I *am*. I want to share with them the love that emanates from me, that comes from the kind of Christians to which I belong. I find that people think they know what Christianity is, but it's not my Christianity, and I'm put into a box before I have opened my mouth.

During my Religion and Theology undergraduate years at the University of Bristol I would tell people what I studied confidently, but when asked if I was a Christian I'd reply, 'Yeah, kind of.' Bristol had a vibrant Christian Union scene that I did not see myself in and did not want to be associated with. I still attended church, quietly, and worked with the Council for World Mission, loudly, but felt unsure in my Christian identity. Most of my friends were met through my Kickboxing and Taekwondo teams and I, for some reason, felt I might be alienated if I was too confident in sharing about being a Christian. It seemed to be something I felt internally, and for a while, that seemed enough. Since moving to Edinburgh, however, and committing to studying World Christianity, I've realized how much of my world-view is shaped by my faith. I love justice. I understand and love my faith by seeing it through the lens of justice. Since immersing myself in political theology, public theology, feminist, queer, Majority World, anti-capitalist theology, 'woke theology' if we must, I've realized how liberating my faith can be. I know how lucky I am to be a member of the United Reformed Church who dedicate a lot of time and resources to their young people. The annual 'Youth Assembly' is a rejuvenating experience for each 14–25-year-old who attends. We are often very few in our local churches and the weekend where we can get together reinforces our identities as young URC Christians. We explore faith together contextually, politically, radically, and talk about the important things our local churches often shy away from. Many denominations do not have a mirror event or youth network. This book can hopefully help any isolated, justice-seeking young person to know that they are not fighting to reshape the Church, fighting to justify their faith in Christ, and balance their often multiple and sometimes seemingly conflicting identities on their own.

The phrase describing us as the 'Missing Generation' has infiltrated denominational reports, research and public language. Phil Knox, head of mission to young adults at the Evangelical Alliance, wrote, 'I believe that we can find the missing generation. We can help a blind generation see. We can see the so-called 'snowflake' generation become a 'youthquake' generation.'[21] Hollie Gard, a Sixth Former at Epsom College, rebuked the term 'snowflake generation':

Presumably, where issues such as racism, sexism and homophobia are concerned millennials have every right to take offence. Whilst debate is healthy, some opinions can be dangerous if they spread inequality, intolerance, or violence. Often individuals are labelled as 'snowflakes' if they take offence at something intended as a joke, yet, even seemingly trivial acts, such as jokes, may become part of a larger, more harmful ethos. In this sense, branding a person as a 'snowflake' for being offended can be seen to be denying them the right to confront inequality and intolerance.[22]

To be a 'snowflake' is to *see* how the trivialization of discrimination legitimizes and normalizes injustice in society. We are not a 'blind' generation. On the contrary, we are a generation that does not blindly follow the status quo but advances to discern Christ's call to do justice in Micah 6.8, and the teaching in Isaiah 1.17 to '[l]earn to do good; seek justice, correct oppression; bring justice to the fatherless, and please the widow's cause'. We see discipleship as to do with being reconcilers and peacemakers for our societies, not as solely or even significantly as individual piety. David Kinnaman supports this notion, arguing that the majority of young people walking away from faith are not putting their relationship with Christ on hold, only their relationship with the conventional forms of church.[23] We are not missing from the Christian participation in Christ's movement and call for wholeness in our world. The Church is often missing, as these chapters will begin to demonstrate.

For the older generations who get stuck into this book, I hope you see the work of some of these young people in your congregations and communities and that it ignites a will to bring more young people into real leadership that brings about change. I was delighted when SCM Press reacted positively to the idea for this book. SCM Press has a wonderful legacy of publishing liberation theologies, the first Christian theology published in Britain about race[24] and the production of radical resources by young people. The Student Christian Movement that birthed the publisher is still providing a home for many inclusive, justice-orientated young students but its space is being squashed in the university sphere. Our desire is to make radically loving Christianity as well known as rigid, traditional, life-limiting, restrictive Christianity. The contributions here begin to outline what that Church might look like in the eyes of young leaders.

Liz Marsh starts us off by exploring climate change, an obvious agenda item for young people. Liz argues that grief is self-satisfying, stagnant and stuck in the past, and for real change to occur we need hope to focus on the now for the future. Liz uses insights from the Majority World who, being closer to the effects of our climate disaster, teach us how to confront this issue selflessly. Chapter 3 explores racial diversity with Nosa Idehen, a Director of the Baptist Church Association of London. Nosa brings her positive experiences of racial integration in churches to argue that real diversity is a necessary gift to the church that cannot be forced by procedures but only by changed hearts through Christ.

Chapter 4 introduces us to Josh Mock, who argues that palatable queer theology is insufficient. He calls for the re-introduction of radical queerness to the Church, exclaiming that queer people are subjected to continuous trauma by having to re-affirm themselves in Christ for the eyes of heterosexual members. Chapter 5 brings Molly Boot, who explores the harmful and difficult topic of trauma related to purity culture in order to question the charged relationships Christians have with their bodies and sexuality. She uses her own experience of feeling fear towards her own body and sexuality and shares how the mystical tradition has helped her reclaim her relationship to her self.

Chapter 6 seeks to take seriously intersectionality in feminism for the Church. Kirsty Borthwick explores how resilient women in ministry have an exhausting task of standing their ground in the current patriarchal climate but also need to be sensitive to the multiple identities of womanhood in our global church. Jack Woodruff, in Chapter 7, conscious that trans theology does not yet have the legacy of other theologies around sexuality, seeks to reaffirm that trans people belong in Christ and God's Church. Jack speaks to any trans peers who may be struggling with their sense of belonging and maps how churches have not done enough to readdress the injustices brought upon trans bodies.

Chrissie Thwaites in Chapter 8 looks at disability justice and its intersection with politics and society. She argues that Christian churches are often blind towards their own ableism and that those with disability need not only to be catered for but need to be enabled to share their gifts fully with their churches, not only supporting them when they are present in the building but also tackling the multiple injustices disabled people face in our society. Chapter 9, written by Anna Twomlow, explores food poverty. Anna combines insights from economics, climate change science, Methodism and politics to argue that food security is synonymous with biblical justice.

Annika Mathews in Chapter 10 explores the relevance of Mental Health for young people. She discusses the wealth of resources we have in the Bible that can help us support others, and seeks to pull the Church away from tepid support towards being completely alongside a person who may be struggling. Shermara J. J. Fletcher writes in Chapter 11 that churches need to allow themselves to be transformed by fully integrating the homeless into their structures. She argues for a radical hospitality that does not stop at seeing people with a need but sees people with gifts.

Sophie Mitchell in Chapter 12 uses her experiences as the University of Bristol's chaplaincy assistant to show how interfaith engagement is an essential practice in the Church. She suggests that friendly events are not enough, and that real relationships can produce social change that can effect all levels of society. Finally, Annie Sharples brings our attention to peace building and her upbringing with the Iona Community. She recounts themes of resilience, patience and bravery and connects the necessity of working for peace with the origins of the Methodist church. The book begins with a powerful poem from Sam, written shortly after the death of George Floyd. It also has a persuasive and dynamic poem from Laura that integrates the Vigil for Sarah Everard, both events that saw young people protest in solidarity.

My generation is not missing from the Church, just sometimes disillusioned with the Church. One young respondent to Steve Aisthorpe's ground-breaking study of churchless Christians stated, 'surely churches exist to promote the gospel and Christianity, but it seems to me that they sometimes fossilize it instead'.[25] I hope these voices from the 'missing generation' will begin to convince the Church at large that the only way forward is a radical, justice-orientated movement. Not to make the Church once again relevant, or to put bums on pews, but to touch lives with the grace and saving power of Christ in a world fallen among thieves (John 10.10).

Notes

1 Please, David and SCM Press.

2 C. McDonald, *God is Not a White Man: And Other Revelations* (Hodder & Stoughton, 2021), p. 101

3 L. Duca, *How to Start a Revolution: Young People and the Future of Politics* (London: Virago Press, 2020), p. 82.

4 J. Burn-Murdoch, 2017, 'Youth turnout at general election highest in 25 years, data show', *Financial Times*, accessed 05/07/2021 via www.ft.com/content/6734cdde-550b-11e7-9fed-c19e2700005f.

5 A. McDonnell and C, Curtis, 'How Britain Voted in the 2019 general election', *YouGov* (19/12/2019) accessed 05/07/2021 via https://yougov.co.uk/topics/politics/articles-reports/2019/12/17/how-britain-voted-2019-general-election

6 75% of 18–24-year-olds voted to remain in the EU. E. Cresci, 'Meet the 75%: the young people who voted to remain in the EU', *The Guardian* (25/06/2016) accessed 05/07/2021 via www.theguardian.com/politics/2016/jun/24/meet-the-75-young-people-who-voted-to-remain-in-eu

7 A. Chakelian, 'Free school meal scandal: Why the government is failing to feed people during the pandemic', *NewStatesman* (12/01/

2021) accessed 07/07/2021 via www.newstatesman.com/politics/health/2021/01/free-school-meal-scandal-why-government-failing-feed-people-during-pandemic

8 A. Romano, 'A history of "wokeness". Stay woke: How a Black activist watchword got co-opted in the culture war', *VOX* (Oct 9, 2020), accessed 26/06/2021 via www.vox.com/culture/21437879/stay-woke-wokeness-history-origin-evolution-controversy.

9 Ibid.

10 Lerner, *Black Women in White America*, p. 575f., as quoted in A. Y. Davis, *Women, Race and Class* (London: Penguin, Random House, 2019 (first ed. 1981), p. 119.

11 A. Boesak, *Farewell to Innocence: A Social Ethical Study on Black Theology and Black Power* (Maryknoll: Orbis Books, 1976).

12 @MatthewPFirth, Twitter reply to @PaulBayes' Tweet, 'Which would you rather? To be Awake? Or to stay proudly asleep?' 20/04/2021.

13 Wokeness and the Gospel Conference, 'Details', accessed 28/06/2021 via www.wokenessandgospel.org/#Details.

14 @HarryLocke Tweet 18/04/2021.

15 @BrexitBatman Tweet 18/04/2021.

16 @DPWBCFC Tweet 18/04/2021.

17 @MisterFister75 Tweet 17/04/2021.

18 See the 'Call for Papers', accessed 28/06/2021 via http://www.rpc.ox.ac.uk/wp-content/uploads/2021/01/Dismantling-Whiteness-symposium.pdf.

19 See W. J. Jennings, *After Whiteness: An Education in Belonging* (Grand Rapids: W. B. Eerdmans Publishing, 2020), pp. 4–10.

20 ECCR, 'Restoring Hope: An Evening in Conversation with Ruth and Rowan', 29/10/2020, accessed 28/06/2021 via www.eccr.org.uk/event/restoring-hope-an-evening-in-conversation-with-ruth-and-rowan-28-october-2020/.

21 P. Knox, 'Finding the Missing Generation', Evangelical Alliance (29/04/2019), accessed 07/07/2021 via www.eauk.org/news-and-views/finding-the-missing-generation

22 H. Gard, 'Is it fair to label millennials the "snowflake" generation?' *Epsom College* (21/05/2021), accessed 07/07/2021 via www.epsomcollege.org.uk/academic/academic-blogs/is-it-fair-to-label-millennials-the-snowflake-generation/.

23 D. Kinnaman, *You Lost Me: Why Young Christians Are Leaving Church ... and Rethinking Faith* (Michigan: Baker Books, 2011).

24 This was J. H. Oldham, *Christianity and the Race Problem* (London: SCM Press, 1924). See K. Clements, *Faith on the Frontier: A Life of J. H. Oldham* (Edinburgh: T & T Clark, 1999) for an in-depth dis-

cussion of Oldham's contribution to thinking about race in missiology and theology more generally.

25 S. Aisthorpe, *The Invisible Church: Learning from the Experiences of Churchless Christians* (Edinburgh: Saint Andrews Press, 2017), p. 194.

2

Climate Crisis: Grief, Anger and Hope as I Look to the Future

LIZ MARSH

In 2050 I will turn 55. In that same year, some climate scientists predict that – if emissions remain at their current level – global temperatures will be on track for a full three degrees Celsius increase compared to pre-industrial times. The consequences of this would be disastrous. At such levels of warming, air pollution will reach dangerous highs in many of the world's major cities. Several crucial climate 'tipping points' will also have been passed, including the vanishing of the world's coral reefs and the melting of the arctic ice sheets, both of which will act as further accelerants of global warming. Likewise, hurricanes and tropical storms will be more frequent than ever before due to higher sea surface temperatures and increased humidity. The impact of all these – and the many other consequences of climate change – will affect almost every aspect of human life, from the food we grow and eat, to the habitability of our cities, to the stability of our global politics.[1] In short, it would be utterly devastating. The above scenario is, of course, a worst-case scenario for 2050 – it's what will happen if we do not reduce carbon emissions any further than we have already. Given the net zero emissions targets that were set at the COP26 summit in November 2021, some reduction in emissions certainly seems likely. Nonetheless, what I outline above gives a brief indication of the potential devastation that the climate crisis might wreak upon our lives and the planet we call home.

When I encounter predictions such as these, or the regular news reports of melting icecaps, fires in California and rising sea levels, I worry for my future and the future of those I love. I am young and I hope that I have many years ahead of me, that I will live long beyond 2050 and well into old age. Yet even as I plan and dream of my future, I find myself plagued with anxieties about the world that I am inheriting. Like many others, both young and old, I find myself grieving; grieving not so much for the past, but for the loss of an imagined future. I have so many questions. What will the world look like when I am old? Will things turn out better than we expect, or maybe even worse? If I have children, what kind of future will I be sending them into? In addition, many climate activists and scientists like to remind us of the brevity of human history when set against the age of the earth. Climate change is a much greater threat to our existence than it is to the planet on which we live. The earth's history long precedes us, and it may also outlast us. We find ourselves confronted, therefore, with our own precariousness, with the certainty that life as we know it cannot and will not continue.

I know that I am hardly alone in my climate-related fears. From talking to my friends, I know that many of them are similarly grieving and anxious about the future. This is borne out by the increasing prevalence of discussions of 'climate grief' and 'eco-anxiety', terms that have been coined to describe the feelings of loss and fear that so many are experiencing. The grieving process has been described as one of 'relearning the world', and climate grief has been conceptualized in the same way: the world is not, and is not going to be, as we imagined, and we must learn to adjust to our new emerging social and ecological reality.[2]

Among young people the sense of urgency regarding the climate crisis is particularly acute: 41 per cent of over 10,000 18–25-year-olds surveyed by Amnesty International in 2019 said that they felt climate change to be the most important issue facing the world.[3] For many of my generation, climate change is the defining problem of our day and age, perhaps precisely because it appears to be such an existential threat to our lives and futures. Many of us are angry, and that anger has been eloquently captured in the words of young climate activist, Greta Thunberg:

> You have stolen my dreams and my childhood with your empty words. And yet I'm one of the lucky ones. People are suffering. People are dying. Entire ecosystems are collapsing. We are in the beginning of a mass extinction, and all you can talk about is money and fairy tales of eternal economic growth. How dare you!
>
> For more than 30 years, the science has been crystal clear. How dare you continue to look away and come here saying that you're doing enough, when the politics and solutions needed are still nowhere in sight.[4]

Thunberg's words contain a clear sense of anger and of hopelessness. The crisis seems to be almost insurmountable and ecological breakdown all but inevitable. If she is correct, then our future of destruction has already been written, not necessarily because of lack of technological or scientific capacity, but as the result of a failure of political will. I am a few years older than Thunberg, but we are not all that far apart in age, and like her I often worry that I will spend much of my adult life dealing with a crisis that is in large part not of my own making. My peers and I do not wish to absolve ourselves of responsibility for the ecological crisis, nor avoid the need to live in ways that are kinder to the rest of creation, but we also know that the destructive patterns of consumption at the heart of this crisis began long before we were born. Furthermore, our concern extends far beyond our own livelihoods and those of the people immediately around us. Instead, there is a deep awareness of the inequalities of climate change and of the fact that it is largely the Majority World that is suffering and will suffer the worst effects of the crisis, even while it is nations in the Western world that have contributed the most carbon emissions. So, many of us are angry; many of us fear for our futures and the future of the planet that is our home. We are grieving; sometimes we are hopeless. In all kinds of ways, we are struggling to relearn the world as it changes before our eyes.

And yet, even as there are moments in which I feel that grief, despair and hopelessness deeply, I am troubled by these feelings and by their implications. More recently, I have found myself called to not dwell complacently in hopelessness, to avoid the alluring temptation of despair, and to remain open to possibility.

The hopelessness I often feel, and that is so pervasive in contemporary climate discourse, assumes the inevitability of the worst possible outcome. I have no desire to deny the reality of the climate crisis, that the situation is serious and it is imperative that we respond accordingly. Nonetheless, it seems to me both unwise and dishonest to declare that we know exactly what the world will be like in 30 or 50 years' time. We can make predictions, of course, and these predictions can be shaped by a wealth of high-quality scientific evidence, but we cannot be certain. So there can be what has been described as a hubris to our grief, an arrogance inherent in our hopelessness, since it assumes a level of certainty about the future to which we simply do not have access.[5]

More troubling still is the corresponding tendency to affix our denial of hope onto the possibility of averting the worst effects of the climate crisis. We find hope in the possibility that we might be able to fix the problem – that with the right technology, enough campaigning, the right politicians in office, our lives might be able to go on almost as normal. The trouble with this is that it has the effect of continually deferring hope into the future. If our hope is dependent upon something that may or may not happen, then we cannot truly realize it in the present. And so for now we remain hopeless, having made hope impossible for ourselves. As such, there is a deep contradiction at the heart of our hopelessness. On the one hand, our hope supposedly rests in our own abilities and is therefore something over which we must have some control. On the other, we find ourselves feeling powerless in the face of seemingly inevitable ecological destruction, not just grieving for the past, but mourning a future that has not yet arrived. We are caught between omnipotence and powerlessness; possibility and impossibility.

In the process of confronting and challenging my despair, I have also discovered great insight in perspectives from the Majority World, and in them the potential to untangle ourselves from the web of contradictions in our hopelessness. If my own despair and hopelessness at the ecological crisis are profound, then I might have expected that those whose lives and livelihoods are already under threat from a crisis that they had no hand in causing would be utterly devoid of hope. This has not been my discovery. Instead, I have encountered resilience, determination and, indeed, hope. None of this is to diminish the deep suffering in much of the Majority World as the result of climate change. In India, for example, more than 45,000 farmers have died by suicide over the last 20 years, largely as a result of the crop failures and economic problems caused by dramatic changes in the climate.[6] Against this backdrop, Anderson Jeremiah, an Anglican theologian and priest from the Church of South India, argues that hope is both essential to life and is discovered and nurtured in community. For him, hope is 'a kind of love', which cannot and must not be privatized less it become deficient. Instead of finding it in wishful thinking, we adopt hope as a moral stance upon the world, and in so doing recognize our own agency.[7] In such a context, in which despair at the climate crisis is proving literally deadly, hope is not a luxury but an urgent, lifesaving necessity.

So, as I have encountered these perspectives offered by people whose experience of the climate crisis is so different to my own, I have been reminded that my sense of hopelessness is not universal, even as it is shared by many. Hopelessness is not the only option, and we do not have to default to it. In this sense, hopelessness is a choice that we make, but then so too can we choose to open ourselves to hope. This choice does not require us to ignore our anxieties about what our collective future might hold. Hope does not require arrogance – a blithely optimistic assertion that everything is going to be OK. Grief and hope can exist together and they do not have to lead us into hopelessness. Hope is not the end-product but rather the beginning, an opening to possibility that allows us to go on in seemingly impossible circumstances.

The importance of hope in the context of possible breakdown has been beautifully summarized by American theologian Catherine Keller:

> To decide that it is too late – that would now be as irresponsible as living like there is no such thing. Opposite modes, but either way, we provide ourselves an alibi, an excuse, an exit from the trouble. To stay with the struggle means to enter not the continuum of dread ... but the wake of mourning, the energy of indeterminacy, and the awakening potential of this now. What matters unconditionally may materialize under the most urgent conditions.[8]

Here Keller is calling us to look beyond our own despair and refuse to accept the inevitability of planetary death, for to fail to do so is to be as complicit in the problem as those who deny that anything is happening at all. We are not asked to deny our grief, nor to pretend that there is nothing to grieve, but it is imperative that we are not consumed by it. As there is a 'moral weight to our grief', then, so too is there a moral necessity to our practice of hope. Part of the task of relearning the world is not to foreclose possibility, not to construct a world without hope by thinking it into existence.

Keller invites us into a new way of being: hope is not just a feeling, something that comforts us in the face of climate-related distress. Instead, hope is an activity, perhaps even a much more fundamental aspect of how we orientate ourselves in the world and towards each other. When we live in solidarity with one another and with the earth; when we refuse to succumb to the temptation of despair, then we live in hope. In this respect we are always learning, always growing. In all our human frailty, our hope may be imperfect, but that does not mean that it is insufficient if it is enough to allow us to go on.

Hope, therefore, is not something that we can ever truly possess. Neither does it rely on certainty, but is rather the ground of possibility. We do not need to be sure what will happen in the future, nor do we need either to decide that it is already too late or claim that nothing can be done. Instead, we can learn to inhabit uncertainty and allow ourselves to live in the present. Perhaps this is not to be feared but can instead be embraced, for it allows us to open our imagination to the unexpected and beautiful. When we do this, we allow ourselves to live in hope in the here and now, no longer deferring it again and again until tomorrow.

In all of this, I also feel increasingly called to relinquish my anger, even as I feel called to channel my passion for climate justice. To be sure, there is a place for righteous anger, but if our anger is directed only at the actions and failures of others then we are failing to recognize our own complicity in the problem. The climate crisis is symptomatic of a much deeper ill, the product of our collective failure to live in a non-destructive relationship with the rest of creation. Even as we seek to modify some of our own patterns of behaviour and consumption – taking care to recycle; reducing our use of animal products and so on – we must thereby recognize ourselves as participants in a capitalist system that has alienated us from the rest of creation and drawn us into destructive patterns of consumption. In relearning the world and our place in it, even as we seek to avoid the hubris of despair and the arrogance of seeing ourselves as in sole possession of the solution, we must also recognize ourselves as participants in the problem. For us to direct all our anger at some other, whoever that other might be, is to refuse to inhabit the discomfort of our own complicity. Even as I sympathize deeply with Greta Thunberg's anger with our global leaders and all those who have participated in decades of denial and insufficient action, so too do I think that it is necessary to move beyond it. If we remain in anger, then we foreclose the possibility of reconciliation with ourselves, with each other, with the rest of creation. We are called, therefore, to move beyond despair, beyond anger, to abandon our hubris and our need for certainty. Hope is not impossible, nor does it need to be endlessly deferred until a tomorrow that may never arrive, but instead we can and must learn to dwell in hope in the present. If there is a 'moral weight to our grief', then so too is there an ethical necessity to our practice of hope.

What does it mean, then, to live in the hope to which we are called? What does it mean for the Church to be a prophetic voice that can challenge the hopelessness that has come to characterize so much of our conversation about the climate crisis? As I have already argued, the problem underlying the ecological crisis goes beyond mere actions to the very heart of our relationship as humanity with the rest of creation. The status quo is rotten to the very core. If we fail to recognize this, then we not only compound our own complicity in the problem, but also close off the possibility of meaningful hope. Even as we seek to move beyond anger, we must refuse to accept the way things are, for to accept them is already to lose sight of the possibility of hope.

What is the role of the Church in all this? In the first place, I would suggest that the Church is called to prophetically articulate an account of hope in the face of what really can seem to be a hopeless situation. This means thinking theologically about climate change and addressing environmental issues in preaching and teaching in order to help congregations and communities to consider their place in the world with respect to the rest of creation. Words are not enough, however. As I have set out in this chapter, hope is found not just in what we say or what we feel, but in finding a new way of living that is in community and solidarity with each other and with the earth. It is not that preaching and proclamation are insufficient, so much as that preaching and proclamation – if they are to be meaningful in this age of despairing uncertainty – must be bound up with action. We must therefore guard against creating an artificial distinction between what we preach and how we act, and learn to recognize our care for creation as central to our faith and its expression rather than additional to it. Neither should issues of climate justice be falsely dismissed as the concerns of a 'woke' generation. All too often, this is used as a way of relegating to the margins of the Church precisely those issues that are (or should be) vital to its witness and calling. If we cannot bring ourselves to do what it necessary to care for the planet and its inhabitants, human and non-human alike; if we cannot summon the courage and the humility to confront our complicity in planetary destruction, then our faith is in danger of being rendered hollow.

To hope, then, we must act, involving ourselves in politics, taking steps to confront injustice, and searching after a better future. As we consider the question of how we might live in hope, it is important to remember that it is insufficient to simply try and reform our current social and economic structures along greener lines. Instead, we must reform the much deeper structural ills at play and recognize that, both collectively and as individuals, we need to fundamentally re-orient our relationship to the earth. More concretely, this means directly confronting the evils of capitalism; joining campaigns for environmental causes and climate justice; divesting from fossil fuels and taking steps to reduce carbon output. We must be unafraid to make radical changes and discontented with any notion of doing the minimum. Though much good work has already been done in this respect, there is still much to do. The task is urgent, but this need not cause us panic, for it is in the undertaking that we find the unfolding of hope. Instead, as we grieve and as we hope, we must not just relearn the world but reimagine and reshape it along lines of love and solidarity with each other and with our planet.

Notes

1 C. Figueres and T. Rivett-Carnac, *The Future We Choose: Surviving the Climate Crisis* (London: Manilla Press, 2020), pp. 23–6.

2 P. Pihkala, 'Climate grief: How we mourn a changing planet', accessed 03/04/2021 via www.bbc.com/future/article/20200402-climate-grief-mourning-loss-due-to-climate-change.

3 Amnesty International, 'Climate change ranks highest as vital issue of our time – Generation Z survey', accessed 10/12/2019 via www.amnesty.org/en/latest/news/2019/12/climate-change-ranks-highest-as-vital-issue-of-our-time/.

4 NPR, 'Transcript: Greta Thunberg's Speech At The U.N. Climate Action Summit', accessed 23/08/2019 via www.npr.org/2019/09/23/763452863/transcript-greta-thunbergs-speech-at-the-u-n-climate-action-summit?t=1623667154042.

5 H. Malcolm, 'Introduction: The End of the World?', in H. Malcolm ed., *Words for a Dying World: Stories of Grief and Courage from the Global Church* (London: SCM Press, 2020), Kindle.

6 A. Jeremiah, 'Farming Grief and Hope', in H. Malcolm ed., *Words for a Dying World,* p. 79.

7 Jeremiah, 'Farming Grief and Hope', p. 85.

8 C. Keller, *Political Theology of the Earth: Our Planetary Emergency and the Struggle for a New Republic* (New York: Columbia University Press, 2018), p. 179.

3

Racial Inclusion: Guidelines to being a More Racially Inclusive Church

NOSAYABA IDEHEN

Being a young Black Christian

First and foremost, I want to highlight that I cannot speak for all Black and minoritized ethnic people because we all have different experiences. My experience as a Black Christian woman in London will be different even to those living in similar contexts, but I aim in this chapter to highlight my personal experiences of racial inclusion and how this can be achieved practically in the Church.

Growing up in a small Baptist church in East London during the very early 2000s, I saw a huge dynamic shift in the demographic of the congregation. A once small church with a majority of elderly white people and few young families soon became very ethnically diverse, with an increase in the number of young people in attendance. My earliest and most memorable instance of racial inclusion that I witnessed was when my dad was nominated to be a deacon by our church administrator. My dad saw this as a call from God into church leadership; he was encouraged the whole way by the administrator and has been heavily involved in most affairs of the church. As a young person, seeing my dad taking up a position of leadership in a nearly exclusively white space was exemplary of how I should not let race become a deterrent, and that ultimately God's will prevails. If a position is meant for me, God will make a way. Ben Lindsay explains in his *We Need to Talk About Race: Understanding the Black Experience in White Majority Churches* that seeing leadership that looks like you is of the greatest importance. He comments about meeting his black mentor Owen in 2000, after growing up in white majority and exclusively white leadership churches, 'For the first time, I had someone leading me who was not only like me in background and upbringing but also allowed me to see someone who was black and leading in a white context.'[1] Unfortunately, there is still a novelty around black leadership in churches. Not all churches collect ethnic data of their ministers, but in the Church of England in 2018, 92 per cent of its clergy, and 94 per cent of its senior clergy were white.[2] Moreover, Revd Dr Andrew Prasad commented at the 2020 Mission Council of the United Reformed Church that at his upcoming retirement, there will be no ethnically diverse Synod Moderators in the denomination.[3] Anthony Reddie also explains that the need for diverse leadership goes past just being able to see someone who is like you, but also to appreciate people who think like you. In his *Is God Colour-Blind? Insights from Black Theology for Christian Ministry* he recalls being overwhelmed by stacks of paperwork at the annual Methodist Conference. This method of producing a 'collective mind on governance', however, elevates one way of knowing and disregards other methods of knowing, namely the proverbial wisdom of African-Caribbean folk, perhaps closer in kind to how Jesus shared his knowledge – through parables and stories.[4] The act of my dad becoming a deacon not only forged a pathway for other black members of the congregation to access leadership but it also enabled other cultural forms of knowing in a leadership that became better representative of the congregation it was serving. It also allowed the daily experiences and struggles of being a black person in a structurally racist society to be voiced and represented at higher levels.[5] The unquestioned experiences and truths of the white male majority – which Willie James Jennings names the epistemology of 'white self-sufficient masculinity' – that prevents alternative ways of being in or seeing the world being taken seriously, are shaken when diversity is introduced.[6]

Thankfully for most people involved in the church, there are ways to contribute other than writing reports. As I grew older in my church, I learned the guitar from my church minister. As an 11–12-year-old girl it was important to have someone like him, who believed in my potential and could spend time nurturing it. Through his investment of time, I finally learned to play the guitar well enough to become the church guitarist. Over 10 years later, I am still in the same church, serving as the only guitarist. It is this kind of commitment towards young people that keeps them invested in their congregation. During the whole process of learning and development, I never once felt that my race was a deterrent to being in the church worship team. The diversity of the congregation and local area was embraced by this minister and the subsequent minister. They both showed me how God can use anyone for his will. Regardless of race, gender or spiritual maturity. Leaders just need to be willing to encourage and nurture people that have skills or potential within the congregation. The church congregation will usually reflect the community it is situated in. If your church congregation doesn't reflect its community, ask yourself why it doesn't.

Further along the line, I went to university. I am trying not to be so proud about the Baptist denomination, but I literally skipped the Christian Union church-hunting event and went to my nearest Baptist church. It mirrored what my home church used to look like before the community became so diverse and developed. Sitting in the pews and singing retro hymns gave me deep feelings of nostalgia, it was a huge reminder of how much things can change in a relatively short period of time. Though the church congregation was a white majority, it did reflect the local population. There was a good spread of different ethnicities, students and elderly people. It made sense given the community context and the fact that the pastor was of Romanian origin. This church actively tried to be multicultural and embraced everyone, especially those in need. This was a wonderful picture of what racial inclusion can look like in a white majority church.

In contrast, I joined a Christian society that was separate from the Christian Union. Most of the members were from the big cities, Manchester and London. It was a majority black society, and felt like a safe space for black Christians. Though we did work with the Christian Union on some occasions; we often held our own events. This society was radical in nature (and name) and it was heavily influenced by the Pentecostal movement. It saw me grow in my own spirituality and personal relationship with God. It was a different experience to that of the church I attended because I was part of the majority; however, I was still serving the same God, just in a different environment. I saw the value of exploring different styles of worship and appreciated the influence of my cultural roots.

In 2019 I graduated with my degree in biochemistry. I came back home to London from Lancaster and the job search was unbelievably difficult. Many doors were closed to me and I didn't know what to do next. A regional minister from the London Baptist Association (LBA) came to preach and advertised a leadership internship that they were running that year for 18–25 year olds. Originally, it did not pique my interest because it was so far afield from what I had studied that I did not feel qualified or able, despite effectively leading worship through music in my church from a young age and being in the leadership of a student Christian society. Nevertheless, my church minister encouraged me to apply. His support really spurred me on to give the application a go and I was accepted! I began to see it as a leap of faith and that God might be directing me towards a path of growth and self-discovery. I've learnt my nervousness at applying is not unique. Ben Lindsay also comments that he has suffered from 'imposter syndrome', where even though he has the qualifications, society's endemic unconscious racism has meant that he had to work harder to achieve a seat at his desired white majority table, and once there, he feels anxious and inadequate because he is different in some way.[7] Even with all my positive influences in my local contexts, reaching beyond them still seemed something that was beyond me.

During this internship I had the opportunity to meet many women in church leadership and especially black women in male-dominated spaces. Seeing their achievements was an encouragement. To see representation in this field, to see women I could identify with opened my eyes to the changes that are occurring in higher church leadership. It gave me a sense of true encouragement. The whole internship empowered me. I felt as though I was being listened to and once again my race didn't feel like an impediment. It was a blessing to be able to give my perspectives and be heard.

There is still a lot to be done to make my positive experiences the normality for all minorities in the Church. This starts with understanding that something is not right with how we approach these issues and putting in steps to change that. The LBA is a positive example. My regional minister and the children and young families lead saw that there was something wrong – there were not many young adults in Baptist Church leadership. To combat this, they created a programme that successfully equips young people with church leadership skills. Karen Campbell, now the United Reformed Church's Secretary for Global and Intercultural Ministries, reflects on how, when joining a United Reformed Church in her mid-20s, she was encouraged into eldership. The church was predominantly black, with a white minister, but the leadership team were mainly black. This encouraged Karen to go into ministry herself. Revd Campbell only began to realize the importance of her journey into leadership at the completion of her training to be a Church Related Community Worker, when she was told she was the first British-born black URC church minister. She explains:

> As I went through my four years of training, most of the people around me were white – the students (of both CRCW and Word & Sacraments), the tutors, the CRCWs already in post; I was conscious of these dynamics, but usually did not

think much about it. Somehow, I just accepted this as the way things were ... One thought I did consciously carry – as a black person in a majority white environment, failure was not an option![8]

The normality of white leadership was imbedded into Campbell's world-view but the encouragement from her black peers, and especially older black women who delighted in her achievements, led her to explore these issues more deeply. The struggle to elevate black voices and experiences is still ongoing in the United Reformed Church, but the story of how Campbell has been able to move from keeping her head down and assimilating to now being in a position to lead the United Reformed Church towards change is inspiring. Even if the change starts off small, it can lead to something a lot bigger. The fact that I am writing this chapter in a book is a testament to that. I have not just done an internship, but have been imbued with confidence that I am leadership material and I do have a calling to my church, my denomination and beyond.

What does racial inclusion look like in the Church?

What does not help

There is a whole paradigm of racial narratives set out for black women. For example, women in general are expected to be nurturing, and black women even more so. Reni Eddo-Lodge comments that black feminists in white feminist spaces were silenced from speaking about intersectionality because it made white women uncomfortable. Black feminism was reduced to 'nothing more than a disruptive force, upsetting sweet, polite, palatable white feminism ... everything was peaceful until the angry black people turned up'.[9] The rhetoric of the 'angry black woman' feeds into the vulnerability of the male ego. Passion, assertiveness and confidence are traits that seek to overthrow systems of violence and injustice that are currently held in place by powerful white men.[10] Being forced to fit into the non-offensive stereotype of the perfect, submissive and small white body by being overly accepting, calm and quiet is to limit our personhood and prevent our elevation. And in the context of leadership, black people must work harder and demonstrate the utmost brilliance to even be considered for the most basic leadership roles, while also being careful not to come across as too confident or powerful. The intersectionality of being both black and a woman makes certain issues in the Church a double whammy. Another reason why this is especially dangerous is because spiritual abuse could easily permeate the situation. Revd Tessa Henry Robinson, who outlines her difficult journey into ministry, explains: 'I began to realize in my deeper conversations with God, that God is not necessarily to be found in every situation, decision and encounter. The reality is that some situations are simply unjust, potentially oppressive and sometimes prejudicial.'[11] The Revd Dr Kate Coleman, previous President of the Baptist Union and chair of the Evangelical Alliance felt called to ministry in a church that did not recognize female leadership. When a breakdown happened in her church, the congregation were happy for her to do the work of the minister as long as she did not have the title. It was not until a white, male leader repented of this view that her gifts were respected.[12] God was with Revd Dr Coleman, giving her the strength to continue his ministry and giving her the skills to convince the congregation of her gifts.

An everyday obstacle for black people is microaggressions, behaviours that have hostile or racist undertones that can be intentional or unintentional.[13] They leave marginalized groups feeling uncomfortable. So please do not narrate to a new young black family that attended the recent service the story of how you went on a mission trip to <insert an African country here>. Depending on what the conversation is about, this could be perceived as a microaggression – a deliberate action that carves out difference. Sometimes harmless words said in passing can be very triggering and leave people of colour (POC) overanalysing what is being said. Microaggressions are a very wicked format of racism that is rife in the UK, not just in the Church but also in the corporate world. It is like slow poison. Over time it can create an environment so toxic that it prevents POC from feeling welcome in certain areas. And POC will end up leaving. The Hope City Church racism row is an example of this, where bureaucratic barriers prevented black people from being part of certain church groups in order to appeal to white Christians.[14]

Grace not Race

The first point: affirmative action. It is a shame that affirmative action is necessary in our church institutions. But this is how Rob Ellis, principal of Regents Park College, Oxford, reacted to one example of affirmative action:

> [W]hen one College head reported on an initiative to change the way we think about these things from the top, and to do it now by appointing at least two people of colour to every senior board and committee, it seemed like a genuine krisis moment ... Waiting for some 'trickle down' or 'percolating up' process to take place prolongs injustice, though it conveniently preserves existing privilege too. Quotas for university places; a curriculum that does not simply justify and entrench whiteness; reserved seats on trustee bodies and the main committees and boards of Baptist Union of Great Britain and College life.[15]

Affirmative action is necessary because white privilege is normalized in all aspects of our society: education, beauty, professionalism, I could go on. What affirmative action does not do is just instate Black and minoritized ethnic people in higher leadership roles. Instead, it corrects our white-centred worldview and bias. Among a pool of multi-ethnic candidates you will find people of each ethnic group that are capable of fulfilling the role that is being recruited. It is not about privileging minorities but instead correcting an unjust system. Affirmative action is a step, not the end, and it needs to be combined with education about unconscious bias, recruiting Black and minoritized ethnic people for the decision-making processes and encouraging Black and minoritized ethnic people to apply for the roles they feel called to. God has instilled gifts into all ethnicities and his grace will hopefully allow us to transcend the current barrier of race that is blinding us as a society.

The second action: tokenism. This is equally as lazy and it also dehumanizes the Black and minoritized ethnic individual by placing the burden of racial inclusion solely on them. They are no longer a teammate but a defence for avoiding racism allegations. They become a token for excusing poor practices and are often given the role of connecting to others in their community rather than the whole team taking on this effort. It pushes the responsibility of interacting with Black and minoritized ethnic people onto the minority person, which negates the purpose of racial inclusion and achieves nothing. In trying to include Black and minoritized ethnic people in more areas of the Church, consider that the grace of God is enough. When we make changes to include others and show God's love, we will make mistakes. Our racial biases, however, should not interfere with or restrict God's will.

Steps to achieving racial inclusion

Reconciliation and re-education

If there are people of Black and minoritized ethnic heritage in the church, are they actively participating in wider church activities? This is a good opportunity to strike up a conversation about people's well-being and whether they feel appreciated as part of the church community. You will also find microcosms in the church simply because people gravitate to people that are like them; race/ethnicity are huge parts of people's physical identity, so it is easier to connect with people that look like you. Have you noticed any such groupings in your congregation and have you engaged with them? You may notice that these cliques form in the church, but remember that we are all human, we are all children of God. So these cliques are nothing to be intimidated by but should be seen as an opportunity to connect with other racial groups. In this way you can become re-educated about race and quench any biases that you may have formed over time. Interaction and re-education work hand in hand as you seek to surround yourself with something you wish to become familiar with. Achieving racial inclusion requires us to be compassionate towards each other and also requires us to be bold enough to reach out of our comfort zone and converse with different people.

Encouraging participation

One thing growing up in church has taught me is that people must be directly approached in order for them to participate in an activity. Sunday morning announcements asking for people to help clear up the churchyard will not work, you will find the same five people doing everything. If you really want Black and minoritized ethnic people to participate in activities or to become leaders, you need to be direct and specific. You need to converse with them and build a relationship. It can be difficult to achieve but it has a domino effect. When one Black and minoritized ethnic person enters leadership it opens up a gateway of possibility for others in the community. Leadership becomes something that can be strived for because a proximal role model has now been created.

Mentorship

Mentors are encouragers. Whether you like it or not, there is always someone that is looking up to you even when you are unaware. They may be older or younger but they see you as an encouragement through your activities or attitudes. Mentorship provides a safe space for growth between the mentor and mentee. For young Black and minoritized ethnic people in particular, a mentor is a huge advantage in their personal development, as young people want to be invested in. The time spent nurturing a young person adds value to them and improves self-esteem.

Lastly, remember that this is everyone's problem. As the body of Christ, if something affects one part of the body it affects the whole body, a body that should reflect the harmony of living well with diversity.

Notes

1 B. Lindsay, *We Need to Talk About Race: Understanding the Black Experience in White Majority Churches* (London: SPCK, 2019), p. 106.

2 H. Farley, 'BAME clergy to receive special mentoring in Church of England bid to boost diversity', *Christian Today* (19/04/2018) accessed 08/05/2021 via www.christiantoday.com/article/bame-clergy-to-receive-special-mentoring-in-church-of-england-bid-to-boost-diversity/128554.htm

3 United Reformed Church, 'Minutes of a virtual meeting of Mission Council held 20–21 November 2020' accessed 08/05/2020 via https://urc.org.uk/images/MissionCouncil/Nov2020/Draft_Minutes_Nov_20_Minutes.pdf

4 A. Reddie, *Is God Colour-Blind? Insights From Black Theology for Christian Ministry* (London: SPCK, 2009), pp. 29–33.

5 See K. Bhopal, *White Privilege: The Myth of a Post-Racial Society* (Bristol: Policy Press, 2018), for an in-depth analysis of enduring structural racism in the UK.

6 W. J. Jennings, *After Whiteness: An Education in Belonging* (Grand Rapids: Wm. B. Eerdmans Publishing Co., 2020), pp. 8–9.

7 Lindsay, *We Need to Talk About Race*, pp. 100–1.

8 K. Campbell and T. Henry-Robinson, 'Cascades of Grace', *Feminist Theology* (Vol. 26, 1, 2017), pp. 47–58, p. 49.

9 R. Eddo-Lodge, *Why I'm No Longer Talking to White People About Race* (London: Bloomsbury Publishing, 2017), p. 164.

10 Eddo-Lodge, *Why I'm No Longer Talking to White People About Race,* pp. 185–7.

11 Campbell and Henry-Robinson, 'Cascades of Grace', p. 55.

12 Lindsay, *We Need to Talk About Race*, pp. 118–19.

13 See C. C. Levchak, *Microaggressions and Modern Racism: Endurance and Evolution* (New York: Springer International Publishing, 2018).

14 S. Beever, 'Sheffield church excluded people of colour from top positions so it would not appear 'too Black', report finds' *Yorkshire Post* (04/03/2021) accessed 22/07/2021 via www.yorkshirepost.co.uk/news/people/sheffield-church-excluded-people-of-colour-from-top-positions-so-it-would-not-appear-too-black-report-finds-3154626

15 R. Ellis, 'A view from Oxford: A reflection on white privilege, and the need for affirmative action', *Racial Justice Blogs*, accessed 30/07/2021 via www.baptist.org.uk/Articles/589079/A_view_from.aspx.

4

Queer, Christian and Tired: Why I'm no Longer Talking to Cishet Christians About Sexuality

JOSH MOCK

I think it's a great way to live ... to fight for yourself, to fight for your friends, to fight for a community of individuals who are sharing your experience and to fight for dignity and a better life, and there will be a tipping point. There will be victories. And they will be joyous. (Peter Staley)[1]

10 December 1989, New York City. For many Catholics who worshipped at St Patrick's Cathedral, nothing unusual was to be expected at that morning's 10:15 Mass, presided over by Cardinal John O'Connor. But church officials and the police were bracing themselves for a challenging morning, having been tipped off about a potential protest at the cathedral.

Cardinal O'Connor was a powerful man and extremely unpopular with the queer community. A deeply queerphobic cleric, O'Connor actively oppressed the queer community and was responsible for a myriad of queercidal actions, including blocking HIV prevention education in New York schools, the passing of New York City's gay antidiscrimination bills, and evicting queer fellowship groups from all Catholic churches under his jurisdiction.[2] Members of the AIDS Coalition to Unleash Power (ACT UP) wanted to confront the Cardinal with the real queer lives his actions were oppressing.

That morning during Mass a crowd of 4,500 protestors coalesced around the cathedral. Chants of 'You say, Don't Fuck; we say, Fuck you' rose like incense.[3] Inside, activists handed out decoy orders of service containing information about ACT UP and HIV prevention. The zenith of the protest was to be a silent 'die-in'. As the cardinal began his homily, protestors lay in the aisle representing nearly 60,000 Americans who had died of AIDS. ACT UP member Michael Petrelis took things a step further: standing on a pew, he blew a whistle and shouted, 'You're killing us!'[4] But another member, Tom Keane, was more daring. As he received communion from the cardinal, he said, 'Opposing safe-sex education is murder' before desecrating the host, crumbling it to pieces and dropping them to the floor.[5]

When I hear stories like this, I can't help but feel that our current approach to queer ecclesial liberation has become too 'decent' and lost the power of actions like those of our queer elders at St Patrick's Cathedral and elsewhere. We have moved away from protests, disruption and acting up, and instead focus on more 'acceptable' forms of campaigning, for example through dialogue with our oppressors. We use Twitter as an arena for criticism of ecclesiastical institutions and those who oppress us online. We write open letters to bishops and church officials calling for change in policy or apologies for harm caused. We take part in facilitated discussion with those who hold 'opposing views' to us, as if queer identities are up for debate, to try to find 'common ground' or ways to 'disagree well'.

The dialogue approach is problematic for several reasons. Dialogue with the Church cannot liberate queer people because dialogue with your oppressor while they are still oppressing you can never bring you liberation. This is the case not only with the Catholic Church, but other (most) Christian denominations too. Take the example of the UK government's LGBT Advisory Panel. Founded by Conservative Prime Minister Theresa May, a politician known for supporting queerphobic policies, including voting against lowering the age of consent for homosexual acts (1998) and against allowing same-sex couples to adopt (2002),[6] it was set up to advise ministers 'on issues and policies concerning lesbian, gay, bisexual and transgender people'.[7] In reality, few conversations took place. In 2021 it was reported that the panel had not met senior government representatives in over a year,[8] and when in 2021 three members resigned over a delay in banning queer conversion practices, the government disbanded the committee rather than act to change the law, although recently they have restarted the investigation process.[9] Oppressive institutions use dialogues and committees to give the impression of listening while absolving themselves from acting on what they hear.

The case of the government's LGBT Advisory Panel is evidence that dialogue with institutions is rarely ever actual dialogue, but rather a tool of oppression used to placate oppressed groups and make them think that they are being heard, and this is often the case in the Church too. Dialogue without justice is monologue and the Church refuses to actively listen to the pain it has caused, choosing instead to cling to its unequal distribution of power.[10] The Church has much to repent of before queer people can engage in just and safe dialogue with it: it has failed to care for queer Christians and people living with HIV infection; it continues to 'legitimize, bless, and activate violence against' queer people;[11] it has unashamedly abandoned the project of human liberation in favour of 'obtaining and maintaining social power'.[12] Until the Church truly seeks forgiveness, repents of its sin and addresses power imbalances, it is not safe nor fruitful for queer Christians to engage in dialogue with it.

Dialogue places the onus on the oppressed to educate and justify themselves to the oppressor, usually to little effect. This is exhausting. Audre Lorde explained this dynamic in a paper given in 1980:

> It is the members of oppressed, objectified groups who are expected to stretch out and bridge the gap between the actualities of our lives and the consciousness of our

oppressor ... Whenever the need for some pretence of com-
munication arises, those who profit from our oppression call
upon us to share our knowledge with them. In other words,
it is the responsibility of the oppressed to teach the oppressors their mistakes ... Lesbians and gay men are expected
to educate the heterosexual world. The oppressors maintain
their position and evade responsibility for their own actions.
There is a constant drain of energy which might better be
used in redefining ourselves and devising realistic scenarios
for altering the present and constructing the future.[13]

When there is dialogue before there is justice, queer people
are manipulated into teaching others about queer issues for
free, despite the vast amount of easily accessible scholarship
that has already been done on the subject. When we do this,
Lorde notes, we enable oppressors to absolve themselves of
any responsibility to educate themselves and make amends for
past failures. Until oppressed and oppressor are on equal foot-
ing, dialogue is impossible.

Another way many queer Christians seek liberation is through
queer theology. As a praxis, it can be extremely creative,
affirming and life-giving. Queer theologies can remind those
who have been rejected by the Church of the radical love that
must be central to Christianity,[14] while exposing the powerful, hegemonic structures in it which require disruption.[15] But
queer theology becomes dangerous when it is used to justify
queerness to our oppressors, often through apologetics and
hermeneutics of 'clobber passages' (the seven biblical passages
traditionally used to condemn homosexuality). Although it
is important to challenge the use of these texts as 'oppressive
weapons with which to accost [queer] communities',[16] such
reclamation and de-weaponization can only go so far. Per-
petual repetition of apologetic arguments to oppressors who
seldom listen is exhausting if not futile. The conversation
stops moving forward and becomes one of 'who can shout the
loudest, the most persuasively and the most powerfully'.[17] We
should also be wary of apologetics that seek to heteronormal-

ize queer identities. Marcella Athaus-Reid and Lisa Isherwood warn that 'terrible is the fate of theologies from the margin when they want to be accepted by the center' because such a desire presents queerness as something to be apologized for and in need of justification rather than celebrated.[18] And when we begin to make our queerness 'decent' for those who oppress us, we begin to assimilate into the heteronormative culture of the Church, conceding to heterosexist society for the sake of acceptability. To avoid assimilating and losing our identity, we must embrace the indecent nature of our identities without heteronormalizing our existence. Marcella Althaus-Reid, the key proponent of indecent theology, made it clear that

> [w]e are always called to confess and repent from normality and its policy of toleration, and we need to stop the circle of the life-energy wasting process of trying to fit into that ideal heterosexual being we should be.[19]

As queer Christians, we must be unapologetic in our queerness. This requires us to do theology from a place of queer celebration rather than a position of queer justification, embracing, not rejecting, the indecencies of our identity.

Not only must we be cautious with the kinds of theological arguments we use, but also be cautious of using theology at all in the struggle for liberation. This is not to say that our liberational approach should be detached from Scripture, but rather that we need to examine the powers behind the discipline and norms of theology. Theology can never exist in a vacuum; 'all theology knowingly or not is by definition always engaged for or against the oppressed'.[20] Marcella Althaus-Reid goes a step further, saying 'every theology implies a conscious or unconscious sexual and political praxis, based on reflections and actions developed from certain accepted codifications'.[21] Whenever we engage in theological discourse, we must be aware that we are also engaging with such power dynamics – power dynamics that have historically been used to oppress, subjugate and condemn queer people. Audre Lorde is clear that 'the master's tools will never dismantle the master's house'.[22] Thus it may be futile to use theology as a tool for queer liberation.

Theology can at times be inaccessible and unrelatable. Goss says that much of theology is 'the produce of people with power and privilege, influence and wealth', possessing 'a partisan bias that renders it meaningful to only a limited audience, particular not universal'.[23] Tonstad believes that queer theology is not exempt from this tendency, saying 'a supposedly queer God might just reflect the concerns of some particular queer people'.[24] Some critics go so far as to say that queer theology is a 'luxury' that only academics can afford to pursue.[25] All this suggests that if queer people can't engage with or relate to theological discourse about our identities, we need to reconsider how liberating theology is for us. I am not saying that we should abandon queer theology – on the contrary, I think it is a vibrant field and many writers are doing important work to bring queer voices to the theological academy as well as opening it up to a wider audience. However, I do believe that our activism needs to be both inclusive and removed from historically oppressive systems, such as academic theology, if it is to be truly liberative. Therefore we should not rely on queer theology alone as a liberative tool but rather use it to inform what we do and how we do it.

So, if dialogue with the Church is currently impossible and (apologetic) theology cannot bring liberation on its own, what is the way forward for queer activism in the Church? I think we need to look back at the actions of our queer elders at places like St Patrick's Cathedral in 1989 and embrace a more transgressive approach. Goss describes transgressive activism as

> the path of direct action, provocation, nonviolent civil disobedience, and offensive parodies … It expresses itself in the refusal to remain silent or to follow proper protocol. It interrupts institutional discourse with angry expletives, shrill noises, a chorus of boos and hisses, chants, whistles, and shouts.[26]

Transgressive activists continue the revolutionary legacy of queer action at Stonewall 1969 and the work of groups such as the Gay Liberation Front, Radicalesbians, and the Gay Activist Alliance. Transgressive activism rejects assimilation into heterosexist institutions and being considered 'acceptable' by them. Transgressive activists don't go through the 'usual channels' to express grievances or to try to change policy, knowing that such procedures are designed to ignore and placate dissenters. To be transgressive is to no longer be concerned if the expression of our queer identities shocks or offends others. It declares, *we're here, we're queer, we will not live in fear*. It says, *I'm no longer explaining myself to you*.

Transgressive activism has biblical foundations. An example found in the Gospels is that of Jesus cleansing the Temple (Matthew 21.12–17; Mark 11.15–19; Luke 19.45–48; John 2.13–16). His overturning of the tables was a demonstrative action, designed to challenge and disrupt economic exploitation and a 'provocative assault on the priesthood and aristocracy'.[27] Jesus' transgressive act, similar in many ways to that of ACT UP in St Patrick's Cathedral, offers a model of transgressive practice for queer Christians. Some may argue that such transgressive activism is 'counterproductive, blasphemous, strident'.[28] However, I see the oppression of queer people by the Church as blasphemous to the gospel message. I think the condemnatory statements made by cishet Christians against queer people are strident. What I think is counter-productive is the conditional acceptance yielded by assimilationist and reformist activists – a conditional acceptance 'purchased at the cost of denying their unique sexual differences, the development of a queer spirituality, and the lack of a whole-hearted commitment to justice-doing for our community'.[29]

Queer Catholics have recently been successful with their transgressive activism. In March 2021 the Congregation for the Doctrine of the Faith, the Vatican body responsible for promulgating and defending Catholic Doctrine, was asked whether the Church could bless same-sex couples. They responded that the Church can't bless same-sex couples, arguing that God 'cannot bless sin'.[30] This enraged many Catholic priests, and the Love Wins movement emerged in Germany with Father Burkhard Hose and Father Bern Mönkebüscher calling for a day of action on 10 May 2021 in defiance of the Vatican teaching. Over 100 priests offered blessings to same-sex couples in a day and it was widely covered by German media. Church officials were outraged but their anger could not stop the demonstration of God's radically inclusive, overflowing, boundless and unstoppable love for all.

I know what it is like to be a closeted queer Christian. You watch all Church statements hawkishly, weighing up what the risk of living authentically could be. To hear that your love is sinful in the eyes of God would be a punch to the gut. To then see hundreds of priests standing up and acting up in defiance and solidarity would be beyond affirming – perhaps even life-saving. There is power in collective transgressive activism. The wider queer Christian community can use Love Win's action as a model for further movements, and all Christians everywhere must stand up to ecclesial injustice with non-compliance.

What transgressive activism looks like for queer Christians in the Church is something we need to discern together and outside the influence of any institutional power. I think there are three principles for discernment to consider:

1. Visibility and presence

'Queer anger is a holy anger. It is time to be angry.' (Robert Goss)[31]

The tragedy of the HIV/AIDS epidemic has shown that with queer issues, silence, apathy and passivity lead to death, while action leads to life. Therefore we must be visible and prominent with our activism in the Church. I worked with other young people in the Student Christian Movement of Great Britain to create a series of videos telling positive stories of queer people in the Church. Entitled 'A More Beautiful Story',[32] the first aim of the series was to centre queer voices and stories in the Church. So often we hear our community spoken about on the lips of cishets rather than ourselves being the voices speaking. This video series was a step in reclaiming the discourse about queer people in the Church. The second aim was to confront our oppressors. The title mocked and played on a video produced by the Evangelical Alliance entitled 'The Beautiful Story', which promulgated mandatory celibacy for queer people and presented queer love as a threat to the Church. Through confrontation and playful yet strategic titles, we increased the visibility of queer people in the Church and showed that we are ubiquitous within it. This goal must be at the heart of our transgressive activism.

2. Confrontation

'Be gay, do crime.' (Queer anarchist slogan)

The German Love Wins Movement is evidence that queer people can confront institutions successfully when they try to attack, condemn and subjugate us. This acting up and confronting of oppressors must become a more common reaction if we are to see true liberation and justice for queer Christians. Christ confronted oppressive powers and defeated their grip on the oppressed through his death and resurrection; we too cannot sit back and allow churches to attack us and give power to those who condemn us. When Hannah Brock Womack was nominated as one of the six presidents of Churches Together in England (CTE) in 2019, numerous member churches of CTE blocked her appointment because she is in a same-sex marriage. This exclusion was passively condoned by the other presidents, who include the Archbishop of Canterbury, Justin Welby, and the Archbishop of Westminster, Cardinal Vincent Nichols, as they 'didn't reach out to [Ms Womack] personally', nor did they publicly condemn the move.[33] Queer Christians should not let stories like these be forgotten nor leave those complicit in such injustices unopposed, and radical interventions are needed to confront the Church's queerphobic actions.

3. Fellowship and community

'Individuals get crushed easily. The community's support and sustaining is crucial.' (Marcella Althaus-Reid)[34]

The charge that queer theology is an academic luxury could also be levied against transgressive activism, as many queer Christians would feel unable to participate in such action, for example priests who would be disciplined for acting against church teaching. However, Stop the Church 1989 and Love Wins 2021 show that there is strength in numbers, and we must discern as a community how we can successfully confront oppressive ecclesial powers in a fruitful and safe way for all involved. We must also care for each other, ministering to each other in prayer, love, sacrament and service, because oppression and the fight against it are exhausting and costly. Queer base communities are a fantastic way of facilitating this, but they are often underfunded and under-resourced. If we seriously want to fight for queer justice in the Church, we need to be more generous towards them with our time, money and attention, and learn from the queer liberation groups before us about how to organize ourselves to make the most impact.

Our current approach to queer liberation in the Church is not working. How many lives must be lost, how many queers rejected, how much grace denied before we accept that assimilation, dialogue, apologetics and compromise will not bring us the freedom we deserve? Queer Christians are tired. We're tired of being asked to 'disagree well' with those in the Church who deny our humanity, as if our identities are up for debate and discussion. We're tired of the notion that there is a conversation to be had about 'discerning a way forward' in matters of sexuality for the Church, when queer theologians have already done the hard work to show that queerness is neither sinful nor incompatible with Christianity. We're tired of hearing monologues about us from cishets in the Church with no lived experience of queerness or the rejection and oppression we experience because of our sexuality. We're tired of compromising on the full celebration of queer lives so that the Church can hold on to its social power, choosing to keep everyone 'happy' (or at least placated) rather than siding with the oppressed and marginalized – the ones who usually get the worse end of the deal. We're tired of waiting for reform in the Church while seeing ourselves further marginalized and oppressed. We're tired of playing according to unjust rules only to see our queer identities hidden and erased. Any continued denial of grace, liberty, equality, inclusion, celebration or love by the Church is a conscious choice to oppress queer people.

I'm tired and there's nothing left to talk about. That's why I'm no longer talking to cishet Christians about sexuality.

Notes

1 P. Staley, 'There will be victories and they will be *joyous*', The ME Action Network, accessed 07/05/2021 via www.youtube.com/watch?v=hsVKOROUNR4.

2 R. Goss, *Jesus Acted Up: A Gay and Lesbian Manifesto* (San Francisco: Harper San Francisco, 1993), p. 54.

3 Ibid.

4 M. J. O'Loughlin, 'Pose' revisits controversial AIDS protest inside St. Patrick's Cathedral', *America Magazine* (2019), accessed 26/04/2021 via www.americamagazine.org/arts-culture/2019/06/21/pose-revisits-controversial-aids-protest-inside-st-patricks-cathedral

5 S. Schulman, 'Interview of Thomas Keane', *Act Up Oral History Project* (24th February 2015), p. 20, accessed 17/06/2021 via http://www.actuporalhistory.org/interviews/images/keane.pdf

6 C. Mortimer, 'All the anti-gay stances Theresa May has taken in her political career', *The Independent* (26/04/2017) accessed 18/07/2021 via www.independent.co.uk/news/uk/politics/theresa-may-lgbt-rights-gay-commons-vote-same-sex-marriage-gay-adoption-tim-farron-a7702326.html.

7 J. Parker, 'Government's LGBT advisory panel disbanded', *BBC*

News (13/04/2021) accessed 18/06/2021 via: www.bbc.com/news/uk-politics-56731460

8 Ibid.

9 A. Allegretti, 'Government disbands LGBT advisory panel after resignations', *The Guardian* (13/04/2021) accessed 18/06/2021 via http://www.theguardian.com/world/2021/apr/13/fears-that-disbanding-of-no-10-lgbt-advisory-panel-will-further-weaken-trust

10 Goss, *Jesus Acted Up*, p. 144.

11 Goss, *Jesus Acted Up*, p. 83.

12 Goss, *Jesus Acted Up*, p. 114.

13 A. Lorde, *Sister Outsider* (London: Penguin Classics, 2019), pp. 107–8.

14 C. Greenough, *Queer Theologies: The Basics* (London: Routledge, 2019), p. 6.

15 Greenough, *Queer Theologies*, p. 34.

16 D. Guest, 'Battling for the Bible: Academy, Church and the Gay Agenda', *Theology & Sexuality* (Vol.15 (1), 2001), p. 77.

17 Guest, 'Battling for the Bible', p. 79.

18 M. Althaus-Reid and L. Isherwood, 'Thinking Theology and Queer Theory', *Feminist Theology* (Vol.15 (3), 2007), p. 304.

19 M. Althaus-Reid, *Indecent Theology: Theological Perversions in Sex, Gender and Politics* (London: Routledge, 2000), p. 131.

20 E. Schüssler Fiorenza, *Bread Not Stone* (Boston: Beacon Press, 1984), p. 50.

21 Althaus-Reid, *Indecent Theology*, p. 4.

22 Lorde, *Age, Race, Class, and Sex*, p. 116.

23 Goss, *Jesus Acted Up*, p. 61.

24 L. M. Tonstad, *Queer Theology: Beyond Apologetics* (Eugene, Oregon: Cascade Books, 2018), p. 84.

25 M. Althaus-Reid, 'The Bi/girl Writings: From Feminist Theology to Queer Theologies', in L. Isherwood and K. McPhillips, eds, *Post-Christian Feminisms: A Critical Approach* (Aldershot: Ashgate, 2008), p. 106.

26 Goss, *Jesus Acted Up*, p. 38.

27 Goss, *Jesus Acted Up*, p. 146.

28 Goss, *Jesus Acted Up*, p. 147.

29 Goss, *Jesus Acted Up*, p. 122.

30 L. Francisco Ladaria Ferrer S J and G. Morandi, 'Responsum of the Congregation for the Doctrine of the Faith to a dubium regarding the blessing of the unions of persons of the same sex' (22/02/2021), accessed 12/06/2021 via www.vatican.va/roman_curia/congregations/cfaith/documents/rc_con_cfaith_doc_20210222_responsum-dubium-unionien.html

31 Goss, *Jesus Acted Up*, p. 177.

32 SCM, 'A More Beautiful Story', https://youtube.com/playlist?
list=PLhD2rr56PEAKfQs_oxM8lRv9NBVp9Jc7S

33 BBC News, 'Church group blocks president due to same-sex
marriage' (26/11/2019), accessed 03/07/2021 via www.bbc.com/news/
uk-england-south-yorkshire-50560663

34 M. Althaus-Reid, *Indecent Theology*, p. 130.

5

When Did I Start Calling My Body 'It'? Purity Culture, Trauma and Learning to Embody Liberation

MOLLY BOOT

When did I start to think of them as somehow apart from me, when clearly this bundle of tissues, fluids, systems and signals are exactly who I am? When we are small, our bodies are watched carefully for signs of growth: how our mouths latch on to our parents' bodies as they feed us, how we track their movements with our eyes, how we begin to move and lift our heads. Our carers are delighted – and concerned – with how our vocal cords begin to resonate, how we start to experiment with our hands and feet, how we roll and play and begin to support our own weight.

For our earliest years we, and those around us, are enchanted by the growth of our little bodies – but for me, and many others, growing up soon becomes a process of disenchantment. If we are lucky, we go to school and are praised or chastised for the growth of our minds. We learn to value our intellect: we are made of memory, skill, experience. Our bodies fade into our peripheral vision, no longer sites of celebration.

From the age of ten, I only remembered my body when she was not what I wanted her to be; when she was too large, or too small, or too soft, or covered by too much hair. I didn't think about her often at all, and when I did there was a tinge of shame, a longing for something different.

At the age of fourteen, I sat in the car on the way to a week of residential rehearsals with my symphony orchestra at a slightly dilapidated boarding school. 'I'll be sending you off to these weeks with condoms soon – when you're ready.' My mum and I have always been very matter of fact about these things. I laughed and assured her that I absolutely did *not* want to have sex until I was married.

Where did that come from? I wasn't a Christian at the time, and I'd read more decent sex education than most teens. But I had absolutely no desire to show my body to anyone else. I barely knew how to be with them by myself, so how could I trust anyone else to be with her? To look at her, or touch them kindly?

At the age of sixteen, I discovered Jesus. I knew, by then, that gender didn't really have a bearing on my crushes. I liked people who were clean and kind, who played string instruments and took school seriously. I liked people who didn't make me afraid to be close to them. I began to explore my body, hoping to find out what made them sing.

I wish I could say that I was at ease with this way of existing; really, I was terrified. My body was unruly – I didn't know what she wanted or needed, or what she was allowed. Desperate for reassurance, I wrote to the pastor of the small, rural Baptist church I'd been attending over the last year:

> I've been so scared that by telling anyone at church that I think I'm bisexual, that I'd lose the love of all of my friends that I rely on so much. Especially with the issues of church membership, I'd hate to lose my place in such an amazing, loving community. I've tried so hard over the last year to suppress this, but I honestly can't. I've cried to God so many times for Him to take away the attraction I feel for some other girls, but nothing's changed. I'm really sorry, I've tried to convince myself that it's a phase, to ignore it and even ask God to change it. I'm still me, I guess, but this is something I'm finding so difficult at the moment, and I don't know what to do.

She replied,

> Lots of young people around your age get confused about their sexuality, and I would advise you to avoid putting any labels on yourself. We'll talk it all through but please rest assured you are not going to be condemned by me or by God. He knows we humans are all imperfect and we all mess up and get confused about lots of things in life, and He loves us anyway.

At the time, I was overwhelmed with relief mingled with foreboding. On one hand, I'd be okay: she wasn't going to condemn me, I wasn't going to lose my church family, and God wasn't going to abandon me. On the other hand, she'd suggested that I was messing up, confused – this was not something good or holy. Visiting my pastor's house after school the next day, I was given these prayers to pray:

> Lord, I renounce all these uses of my body as an instrument of unrighteousness and by doing so ask You to break all bondages Satan has brought into my life through that involvement. I confess my participation. I now present my body to You as a living sacrifice, holy and acceptable to You, and I reserve the sexual use of my body only for marriage. I renounce the lie of Satan that my body is not clean, that it is dirty or in any way unacceptable as result of my past sexual experiences. Lord, I thank You that You have totally cleansed and forgiven me, that You love and accept me unconditionally. Therefore, I can accept myself. And I choose to do so and to accept myself and my body as cleansed. In Jesus name, I pray, amen.

> Lord, I renounce the lie that You have created me or anyone else to be homosexual, and I affirm that You clearly forbid homosexual behaviour. I accept myself as a child of God and declare that You created me in my natural gender to worship you. I renounce any bondage of Satan or attachments of evil

spirits that have perverted my relationships with others. I announce that I am free to relate to the opposite sex in the way that You intended. In Jesus' name, I pray, amen.[1]

The contradictions were overwhelming: I wasn't unclean, God 'love[d] me and accept[ed] me unconditionally', and yet, my body was lying to me. Satan and 'evil spirits' seemed to be involved too, lying about my sexuality and about my unacceptability, 'perverting' my relationships and holding me captive. How could these things all be true at once? Were these forces really at work in me?

And with that, my relationship with my body crystallized – as it does for so many Christian teenagers – into one based on the fear and expectation of betrayal. She – 'it' – was the domain of temptation, even satanic deception – to be prayed against, suppressed and ignored.

There is plenty of excellent and sobering writing out there about the history, rhetoric and experience of 'Purity Culture' – the heady atmosphere of blame and responsibility surrounding young people's sexuality, particularly in UK and US evangelical contexts.[2] In youth groups and Bible camps throughout the Global West, fear of our sexual bodies is built on metaphors of wilting flowers, or pieces of chewing gum sullied as they are passed from person to person. The more people who handle the flower or gum, the dirtier and more 'used up' they become; the lesson, of course, is that this is what happens to our bodies, or the so-called 'gift of virginity', with each sexual experience. By the time we meet our God-ordained spouses, we are too dirty to be desired. Our purity has been lost.

These object lessons make our bodies 'its', rather than 'thems' – items to be used up rather than our very selves. These metaphors got under my skin and made it feel as though that skin itself was wilting, dirty, whenever I or anyone else tried to love it.[3]

Siblings in Christ: these are not *our* metaphors. They are not inherited from a rich tradition of faithful worshippers reflecting on their relationship to God and their fellow humans. They were formed in the crucible of a shrinking twentieth-century church panicking that their young people were lost to 'the world' and that their bodies, minds and spirits needed to be controlled. These images, shot through with shame, have taken many of us captive.

So where might we turn for alternative images? Images that are more liberating, loving and faithful to our tradition?

The rich physicality of the Hebrew Bible is no surprise to Jews, but Christians have a tendency to blush through the sex scenes and fast forward to the Pauline epistles. We have the immense privilege of sharing a story in which God breathed life into dust – *adām* – and made it sensual. In the Torah and the Prophets, we have a witness to the costly gift of sexuality: we see pleasure, shame, joy, pain, childbearing, child loss, sex work, rape, passionate love and infidelity. Sensual images of fruit, water and oil describe the risk and blessing of desire, as Scripture describes the holy, foolish and evil exploits of humans in the pursuit of love. And, of course, our canon of Scripture includes the Song of Songs: an evocative collection of erotic verse in which lovers rejoice over each other's bodies.

In order to justify its status as Scripture, allegorical interpretations have been laid over the Song; from Rabbi Aquiba's assertion that it is a description of the relationship between Israel and the Divine Presence, the *Shekinah,* to Origen's insistence on the Song as an allegory for the marriage between the Bride – the Soul or the Church – and Christ. Origen warns his readers of the danger the Song of Songs poses to those who do not take this spiritual, allegorical approach:

> For he, not knowing how to hear love's language in purity and with chaste ears, will twist the whole manner of his hearing of it away from the inner spiritual man and onto the outward and carnal; and he will be turned away from the spirit to the flesh, and will foster carnal desires in himself, and it will seem to be the Divine Scriptures that are thus urging and egging him on to fleshly lust![4]

But what if our Scriptures *are* 'urging and egging [us] on' – to reconnect with our bodies; to connect with other bodies; to awaken fleshly, Godly desire? Strangely enough, Calvin foreshadowed a turn from purely spiritual allegory to an approach that made room for the Song to express both divine inspiration and human love.[5] A 'literal' interpretation of the Song of Songs (notably the kind of interpretation that churches promoting purity culture often prefer), leaves no room for uncertainty: 'A whole book extolling the beauty of human sexual love! How could Scripture more forcefully proclaim that human sexuality is not cheap, ugly and evil, but beautiful, wholesome and praiseworthy!'[6]

These stories and songs are far from perfect blueprints for a liberative experience or understanding of our sexuality. Women are marginalized and abused. Sexual minorities are shunned or, more often, absent. Purity laws predate purity culture with their insistence on cleanliness, and have themselves led to the denigration and control of women's, queer and disabled bodies. But, these messy stories of the power, volatility, risk and joy of human sexuality do, at the very least, prevent us from seeing our bodies as 'it', 'other', 'object'.

We are *adām*, the ground itself, each of us inspired by the breath of God. The creation story in Genesis 2 demonstrates our earthy embodiment in stark terms. Our bodiness is not an optional extra; this is again evident in the Gospel accounts of Christ's incarnation, life, passion, death and resurrection. God not only inspires bodies, but chose to be one. Our tradition does not allow us to lose sight of our flesh to focus on our spirits; so we must learn to live well with our bodies.

My own sexual-spiritual revolution came from the Christian mystical tradition – which, again, is far too complicated to be held up as a map to sexual liberation. While I wish that the mystics that I have fallen in love with over the last few years were perfect protofeminists, leading the charge on sexual liberation, in reality many had conservative understandings of gender roles, and several wrote enthusiastically on bodily and sexual self-denial as an essential part of ascetic and contemplative practice. Nonetheless, I have been surprised and encouraged to find out that mysticism has more to do with bodies than I had expected. I had anticipated tales of the mortification of the flesh for the sake of the exaltation of the mind. Instead, the tales of ecstasy that I encountered were more holistic, more fleshly.

Take Hadewijch of Brabant, a thirteenth-century beguine and mystic. Church historians who like to talk about sex often point to her, and our colleagues roll their eyes – but I think there's good reason to mention her here. Hadewijch talks about experiencing God as *minne* – 'not God, or Christ, or Divine Love ... *Minne* is an experience, the way in which the soul experiences its relation to God, a dynamic experience of relationship'.[7] It seems clear to me that this powerful experience of relationship with the divine captures not only her soul, but all her faculties: her mind and body, too. Famously, Hadewijch was overwhelmed by a vision one Pentecost in which her 'heart and [her] veins and all [her] limbs quivered with eager desire ... it seemed to [her] that [she] did not content [her] Beloved, and that [her] Beloved did not fulfil her desire'. She sees Christ come to her as a man, 'wonderful, and beautiful, and with glorious face', who gave himself to her in the sacrament. She describes 'melting away' into Christ:

> After that he came himself to me, took me entirely in his arms, and pressed me to him; and all my members felt his in full felicity, in accordance with the desire of my heart and my humanity. So I was outwardly satisfied and fully transported. Also then, for a short while, I had the strength to bear this; but soon, after a short time, I lost that manly beauty outwardly in the sight of his form. I saw him completely come to nought and so fade and all at once dissolve that I could no longer recognize or perceive him outside me, and I could no longer distinguish him within me. Then it was to me as if we were one without difference. It was thus: outwardly, to see, taste, and feel, as one can outwardly taste, see, and feel in the reception of the outward Sacrament.[8]

To describe this experience between Hadewijch and Christ as 'sexual' or 'erotic' is not to suggest that somehow it is not holy: only that her body, and his incarnate, sacramental body, were clearly indistinguishable from each of their spirits in this intensely physical *and* spiritual moment of union.

Hadewijch is far from alone in her blending of the language of sensuality with the language of mysticism; it is hardly surprising that overwhelming experiences of divine love have needed to share the grammar of sexuality from the Song of Songs with medieval mysticism, to modern charismatic evangelicalism. The very church tradition that alienated me from my body, that created the metaphors that make our bodies dangerous or damaged 'its', inherits a mystical, erotic language of worship and adoration. While I learnt to distrust my body in those spaces, there was a glimmer of hope that she could be caught up by God in ecstasy. In the song 'How He Loves', David Crowder Band sings the line 'He is jealous for me...'. This song is often ridiculed as a classic example of 'Jesus is my boyfriend' worship song writing – but the medieval mystics trademarked 'Jesus is my boyfriend' – or rather, bridegroom – first! Like Hadewijch, David Crowder extols the beauty of God and desires to be overwhelmed by union: 'bending beneath' the very weight of the Divine presence, getting lost in the eyes of Christ, his heart racing at the 'kiss' that joins heaven and earth. Body and spirit become indistinguishable as the worshipper is joined in love to the Lover of all creation. The semantics of sex and charismatic and mystical spirituality intertwine, as they seek to capture the very heights of human experience, as we live between desire and satisfaction.

It is often said that evangelical traditions express and teach their theology in their music: and so I wonder what would happen if the churches of my youth taught the sexual ethics suggested by their worship songs? If they taught that our sexual bodies reveal divine love in their eroticism, not just in their chastity?

I remember one of my university supervisors mischievously asking her first-year undergraduates whether it's okay to love

God erotically and watching them shift uncomfortably, looking for an inoffensive answer. The witness of the medieval mystics, and of much modern charismatic worship music, is to my mind a resounding 'yes'. Our erotic bodies are agents of revelation, in their experiences of desire, pleasure and fulfilment, as they experience union with themselves, with others and with God. Our tradition bears witness to this holy, liberative view of our corporeality and our sexuality. We are not mere objects. That teaching that makes our bodies crumpled flowers, chewed gum and instruments of corruption is a denial of what it is to be human – to participate in the bodily resurrection life of Christ, and to experience love of God and neighbour with all our senses.

> Holy Spirit of God,
> Jesus, the body of God,
> God, the parent who birthed us –
> Give us back the gift of our bodies.
> Forgive us where we have objectified ourselves and others.
> Let us share in the pleasure you take in creation.
> As we meet ourselves, others and you,
> let us experience the joy of loving union
> with all that we have, and all that we are.
> Amen.

Notes

1 N. T. Anderson, *A Way of Escape: Freedom from Sexual Strongholds* (Eugene, OR: Harvest House Publishers, 1994), p. 14.

2 I strongly recommend you seek out Dr Katie Cross's powerful chapter, 'I have the power in my body to make people sin' in *Feminist Trauma Theologies*, ed. K. O'Donnell and K. Cross (London: SCM Press, 2020). Other more detailed examinations of Purity Culture include: C. Gardner, *Making Chastity Sexy: The Rhetoric of Evangelical Abstinence Campaigns* (Berkeley, CA: University of California Press, 2011); D. E. Anderson, *Damaged Goods* (Nashville, TN: Jericho, 2015); L. Kay Klein, *Pure* (New York, NY: Touchstone, 2018); and

S. Moslener, *Virgin Nation: Sexual Purity and American Adolescence* (Oxford: Oxford University Press, 2015).

3 In writing this chapter, I have wondered whether Purity Culture could be identified outside of European and American contexts, overshadowed as they are by white supremacy. Purity culture relies so heavily on 'whiteness' as a metaphor, and is so entrenched in misogynistic and white supremacist understandings of what bodies should be and how they should behave, that I think conservative global majority sexual ethics would require a different approach, and far more comprehensive examination than I am able to offer.

4 Origen, *The Song of Songs Commentary and Homilies*, trans. R. P. Lawson (London: Longmans, Green & Co., 1957), p. 22.

5 R. M. Davidson, 'Theology of Sexuality in Song of Songs: Return to Eden', *Andrews University Seminary Studies* (Vol. 27 (1), 1989), pp. 1–19, p. 4.

6 Ibid.

7 Norbert De Paepe, *Hadewijch Strofische Gedichten. Een studie van de minne in het kader der 12' en 13' eeuwse mystiek en profane minnelyriek* (Ghent: Koninklijke Vlaamse Academie, 1967), p. 331.

8 Hadewijch, 'Vision 7' in *Hadewijch, the Complete Works*, ed. C. Hart and P. Mommaers (New York: Paulist Press, 1980).

6

Comfortable Feminism is Not Enough: Following Christ's Call for Abundant Life

KIRSTY BORTHWICK

So again Jesus said to them, 'Very truly, I tell you, I am the gate for the sheep ... I came that they may have life, and have it abundantly.' (John 10.7, 10)

As a young Christian woman, I dream of a church in which all gatekeeping is modelled on Christ for the flourishing of all (because a church which denies gatekeeping at all is dangerously naive of its power).

As a young woman preparing for ordained ministry in the Church of England, I long for the recognition of the gifts of women in all manner of lay and ordained roles. As someone who has tolerated disparaging and sexist comments, and as a woman whose heart breaks to see anyone experience similar, whatever their theology or identity, I'm desperate for a church in which there is no need to dread conversations around gender. As a passionate ecumenist, with friends in a number of churches who cannot or will not receive my ordained ministry, I yearn deeply for the flourishing of all God's children while taking seriously the pains of all that separates and disempowers us.

I am a young Christian feminist because God calls us all into abundant life. Christian feminism insists, with a variety of emphases, that without the liberation of women our understanding of the abundance of Christian life is incomplete.

At the same time, I'm wary of the feminist label. Feminism has a dangerous tendency of leaving people behind. When women 'won the vote' in 1918 this only applied to women over the age of 30 with property (in comparison to any man over 21). It was not until 1928 that parity with male suffrage was achieved. Today's feminism is also far from perfect. Important progress in trans rights continues to be hindered by Trans-Exclusionary Radical Feminists (TERFs) who refuse to recognize that the flourishing of ciswomen cannot be at the expense of our trans and nonbinary siblings. Womanist Theology, which is reaching an increasingly wider audience, rightly recognizes the particular experience of Black women and challenges feminism's tendency to be little more than white feminism, dangerously unaware of its own skin. If feminism does not seek the flourishing of all women, we can no longer consider it worthy of its name.

And so, as I reflect on my experiences as a young Christian woman who is also white, able-bodied, cis, straight and middleclass, I'm insistent on two things: first, that feminism on its own can never be truly liberating; and second, that we've still got work to do. I leave aside wider questions of Christian feminism – like feminist readings of Scripture, feminist understandings of God, or the question of whether women can be ordained – not because these are unimportant, but because that work is readily available elsewhere. Here, instead, I share my concerns and my hopes as a young woman on the cusp of committing to a lifetime's ministry in the Church of England, with the anticipation that they will provoke but perhaps also encourage and inspire.

Feminism is not enough: women and their unique identities

If anything should remind us that feminism on its own is not enough, it should be this book's title. The word 'woke' is often used today as a broad clarion-call or insult in our so-called 'culture wars'. However, woke origins are far more specific, arising from the lives of black Americans, with notable uses of the Harlem slang in Lead Belly's 1938 Blues song 'Scottsboro Boys' and in the title of William Melvin Kelley's 1962 essay 'If You're Woke You Dig It'. More recently, it was two black women meeting in Los Angeles in the early 2000s that marked the beginnings of 'woke' in the mainstream. Georgia Anne Muldrow's lyrics and Erykah Badu's voice, brought together in the song 'Master Teacher', aspired for resilience in the wake of inequality with the cry: 'I'd stay woke.' A few years later #staywoke made its global debut as a rallying cry of the Black Lives Matter Movement.[1]

As a white woman, I'm not woke. I'm passionate about social activism and particularly the anti-racist cause, but my life circumstances don't demand that I stay woke. Yes, good allyship demands paying attention and active response. But an inescapable need to stay woke is not my experience and it does not shape my immediate identity. And that is why feminism alone is not enough, because no one is simply a woman. We each share in various demographics and characteristics, but our various contexts and experiences give rise to unique identities.

This is what language of 'intersectionality' addresses. The term, first coined by legal scholar Kimberlé Crenshaw in 1989, refers to the particular challenges or privileges faced at the intersection between different aspects of our identities.[2] Crenshaw's article focuses on a number of particular prejudices exhibited on Black women which demand multi-axis analysis. She discerns that addressing the needs of Black women cannot be done through an analysis of either race or gender alone. We are all multidimensional people and the differing combinations of those dimensions cannot be ignored. 'Ah, but you're just spouting identity politics', my critics might cry. So-called 'identity politics' gets a lot of stick in Christian circles, occasionally for good reason but often as a result of misunderstanding. By drawing attention to intersectionality, I do not wish to deny our primary Christian identity in Christ.

As I continue to discern my calling to ordained ministry, one moment that shapes that above all others, a moment not even limited by the fact I cannot remember it, occurred on one sunny afternoon in June 1992 when I died and rose with Christ. I am defined by my baptism. Who I am in Christ *is* who I am. But in baptism, Christ calls us by name. In baptism, in Christ, I am Kirsty. And Kirsty is a white, straight, woman whose life thus far has shaped me to be British, able-bodied and middle-class.

In a press release during the work of the Church of England's recent Anti-Racism Taskforce, the Taskforce made these comments on its work:

> In seeking to address the sin of racism in our church we do so seeking to follow a biblical imperative which we share with all followers of Christ. Our work is not a battle in a culture war but rather a call to arms against the evil and pernicious sin of racism. Our mandate flows not from identity politics but from our identity in Christ. This is our primary identity and it is in the character and being of Christ that we find the reason and motivation to combat racism.[3]

My understanding of my own identity, and the ways in which it both underprivileges me (as a woman) and makes me complicit in many other injustices, echoes this. I understand who I am, in all manner of multifaceted ways, only in the light of who I am in Christ. But at the same time, none of us is a vacuum, filled by Christ at baptism. We are created uniquely, each of us 'wonderfully and fearfully made' (Psalm 139.14) in all our complexity. We are unique creatures, known and loved by God and called into the Christian life not to abandon what we are, but for what we are to be made perfect, to be honoured, to be glorified. Each of us is shaped in ways beyond our full reckoning, by our contexts and experiences. We are promised that all that we are is not lost in Christ, but found.

Here lies an opportunity for the churches to proclaim and enact good news in the world, not simply borrowing from secular principles, but shaping them theologically. Christians who call themselves feminists are not an example of the

Church being pulled into a 'culture war'. Feminist work has the potential to be one of the many outpourings of the Church's mission in the world. The Anglican Communion's Five Marks of Mission include (in its fourth mark) an insistence that 'the mission of the Church is the mission of Christ ... to transform unjust structures of society, to challenge violence of every kind and pursue peace and reconciliation'.[4] Feminism is a part of that process.

Work still to do: young women in the Church of England

Of course, the churches should not challenge society without recognizing where they too may be at fault. This is particularly important when it comes to mission in and among younger generations. Young people are notoriously good at spotting hypocrisy.

In this, the second half of this chapter, I consider the implications of feminist thinking in the life of the Church of England. I focus on the Church of England because it is here that I minister and thus it is this aspect of the life of the Body of Christ that I most know. If you are a member of another tradition or denomination, or from elsewhere in the Anglican Communion, I invite you to ask similar questions of your own particular ecclesial home. It can be all too tempting for many in our churches, especially those churches which allow for the ordination of women, to assume that our work towards women's equality is done. And so, above all, I invite you to ask, 'What has been achieved?' and 'What work is there yet to do?'.

In the Church of England, we have three orders of ordained ministry: deacons, priests and bishops. As of 17 November 2014, women can be ordained to all three of these roles. I was born in November 1991. By coincidence, because of when General Synod meets, November has been a significant month in the progress towards women's access to ordained ministries in the Church of England.[5] In November 1986 provision was made for women to be ordained as Deacons. This had been in place for five years at the time of my birth. In 1993, just days before I turned two, provisions were then made for women to be ordained as priests. Many years later, as I began to explore a call to ordained ministry, I was flabbergasted to learn that this change had taken place in my own short lifetime.

I remember November 2012 very well. Just turning 21 years old, and as yet possessing absolutely no interest in ordination, I had reached my final year of study as an undergraduate. As a young theologian, and a woman who had always called the Church of England home, I suddenly found myself deeply interested, invested even, in the workings of General Synod. The possibility of ordaining women as bishops was on the horizon. The moment felt significant. I abandoned important revision and ignored impending essay deadlines to follow the Synod proceedings. When the proposed legislation was not passed, I wept. I didn't really know why, but I knew I felt wounded. I remember this moment more than I remember hearing the news, two years later in November 2014, that new legislationure had been agreed and women could now be bishops. I rejoiced in that moment; I still do. But the 'no' of 2012 will always shape me.

Women in the Church of England can now be ordained to all orders of ministry. In the wake of God's calling there is no longer a legislative glass ceiling. And yet, there is still work to do. Indeed, the 'no' of November 2012 has placed the Church of England in a unique position which precisely *demands* that there is always more work to do.

In response to the 2012 vote, and in order to pursue fresh legislation which would protect the theological convictions of those against the ordination of women while enabling the ordination of women to be recognized in law, the Five Guiding Principles were introduced. It is in the light of these principles that the legislationure to allow for the ordination of women as bishops was passed in 2014. The principles are to be read and held together in tension, and consciously recognize both the depth of disagreement in the Church of England over women's ministry and a passionately held desire to 'stay together' as one church. Assent to these principles is now a requirement for all seeking ordination. Given their importance, I quote them here in full:

1 Now that legislation has been passed to enable women to become bishops the Church of England is fully and unequivocally committed to all orders of ministry being open equally to all, without reference to gender, and holds that those whom it has duly ordained and appointed to office are true and lawful holders of the office which they occupy and thus deserve due respect and canonical obedience.

2 Anyone who ministers within the Church of England must be prepared to acknowledge that the Church of England has reached a clear decision on the matter.

3 Since it continues to share the historic episcopate with other Churches, including the Roman Catholic Church, the Orthodox Church and those provinces of the Anglican Communion which continue to ordain only men as priests or bishops, the Church of England acknowledges that its own clear decision on ministry and gender is set within a broader process of discernment within the Anglican Communion and the whole Church of God.

4 Since those within the Church of England who, on grounds of theological conviction, are unable to receive the ministry of women bishops or priests continue to be within the spectrum of teaching and tradition of the Anglican Communion, the Church of England remains committed to enabling them to flourish within its life and structures.

5 Pastoral and sacramental provision for the minority within the Church of England will be made without specifying a limit of time and in a way that maintains the highest possible degree of communion and contributes to mutual flourishing across the whole Church of England.[6]

These principles demand our active attention and assent. Together they speak of a definite decision made, but also of continued ambiguity. To take up language used in the ecumenical movement, this implies that the principles need always to be 'received'. They are not simply a statement of facts, but a statement of intent.

The Five Guiding Principles are controversial, not least because they refuse to remove difference. Many women (and men) in the Church of England, older than me, fought hard for the ordination of women over many decades and I understand why for many the Five Guiding Principles are a painful compromise. In the wake of continued insults and sexist remarks and a long history of being told 'no', mutual flourishing is not something that appears in an instant. The wounds run deep. I would not want to undermine that pain in any way. And if we claim 'mutual flourishing' is easy or immediate we do precisely that.

But I am willing to assent to these principles, in fact I am pleased to, because at their best they call us to the long pursuit of mutual flourishing. At their best, these principles demand that our work towards women's equality, and our pursuit of deeper fellowship with those who do not believe in the ordination of women, has only just begun. They ask us to pursue an active relationship with one another in among the messiness of our difference.

Already the Five Guiding Principles have shown themselves to be messy. This came to the fore in January 2017 in the multifaceted reaction to Bishop Philip Burnley's nomination as Bishop of Sheffield. Bishop Philip is one of a number in the Church of England who do not receive the ordained ministry of women, and thus his nomination was contentious. After considerable public debate, frustration and pain experienced by women and their supporters and conservative parties alike, Bishop Philip withdrew his acceptance of the nomination.

These events underwent an Independent Review in the conclusions of which it was noted that we should not assume the

Five Guiding Principles had failed. The Independent Reviewer concluded:

> The Guiding Principles are simply that – guiding principles. They are meant to be applied and their implications worked out in the context of particular circumstances.[7]

In other words, the events surrounding Bishop Philip's nomination point precisely to the need to engage with these principles, particularly in the most complex and vulnerable of circumstances. And that work has begun. In the years since, Women and the Church (WATCH) and the Faith and Order Commission of the Church of England have both produced dedicated resources exploring the Five Guiding Principles.[8] Commentary material is also available from Forward in Faith.[9]

But the Five Guiding Principles are not enough alone. The 'flourishing' they call for must mean more than simply the right for women to be ordained. And here we come again to the multidimensional nature of each of our identities. If we are not flourishing across the intersections of our different contexts, arguably we are not truly flourishing at all. We need to ask questions, then, about the flourishing of women – and nonbinary persons and transmen – who fall pregnant. Policies for parental leave are handled by each Diocese, which can lead to differences in expectations. Explicit guidance on supporting pregnant ordinands was only issued in March 2020, until then leaving those in training in a vulnerable position.[10]

Moreover, we need to ask questions about the flourishing of young women in ordained ministry. WATCH, in their 2020 report, noted the tendency for women to enter training later in life – in 2020 only 33 per cent of ordinands under the age of 35 are women. This will have an effect both on the culture of various training contexts, and on how many women have sufficient longevity of experience to take up senior church roles. As the report notes, 'until this pattern is acknowledged it will not be possible to plan strategically, and use money strategically, to start to remove this imbalance'.[11]

We also need to ask urgent questions about the flourishing of UK Minority Ethnic women in the life of the church. In the otherwise wide-ranging recommendations in the recent Anti-Racism Taskforce Report, none pertain particularly to women. Taking seriously Crenshaw's work on intersectionality means we must ask what we might be missing about the particular challenges faced by UKME women in the Church of England. Indeed, the same lack of specially commissioned research applies to the lives and ministries of many other women. What specific challenges faced by disabled women, and working-class women, and lesbian, bisexual or transgender women, are we missing? How might these experiences be intersecting in ways to which, as a church, we are not paying sufficient attention?

And we urgently need to address those aspects of the church's life which not only inhibit the flourishing of women, but which more generally contribute to subjugation and abuse. In her assessment of power and abuse in the Church of England, Fiona Gardner notes the ways in which 'toxic masculinity' (those aspects of stereotypical masculine culture which damage all genders alike), class dynamics and an apparently benevolent (even sanctioned) form of sexism enables a culture of secrecy in which abuse continues unchallenged.[12] If we fail to address problematic systems as they appear in the Church of England – including structures of patriarchy – it is not just women who suffer. Again, the flourishing or non-flourishing of the few is bound up with the flourishing of all.

And, finally, we need to ask questions about the flourishing of lay women in the life of the Church of England. Too much of the conversation about women's ministry has focussed on the ordained life. This focus has been important. Ordained women are a relatively new phenomenon and, as we have seen, the Five Guiding Principles commit us to further work to be done in exploring the implications of women's ordination. But there are far more lay women in the church than there are women who are ordained, and they are arguably the backbone of the church's daily life. Why then is there no substantial mention of gender in the Church of England's latest report on lay ministry, 'Setting God's People Free'?[13] What models of leadership are we over-applauding in such a way that we then minimize the importance of roles often inhabited disproportionately by women: those who welcome, those who arrange flowers, those who offer their gift in administration? Again, what or who might we be missing?

> So again Jesus said to them, 'Very truly, I tell you, I am the gate for the sheep ... I came that they may have life, and have it abundantly.' (John 10.4)

I continue to dream of a Church which recognizes its gate-keeping, owns it, and seeks thereby to uphold the flourishing of all. The Church of England has made remarkable progress with regards to women's ministry in recent years, albeit I am disappointed that progress took so long to begin. But we must not forget that there is work still to do. We must not fall into the trap that feminism so easily falls into, of failing to recognize the complexity of women's identities, or of leaving some women behind. Any church that refuses to succumb to these things is a church I can be proud to serve.

Notes

1 For an overview of this development of the word 'woke' see www.okayplayer.com/tag/the-origin-of-woke, accessed 28/04/2021.

2 K. Crenshaw, 'Demarginalizing the Intersection of Race and Sex: A Black Feminist Critique of Antidiscrimination Doctrine, Feminist Theory and Antiracist Politics', *University of Chicago Legal Forum* (Vol. 1989, (1), Article 8). Available at: http://chicagounbound.uchicago.edu/uclf/vol1989/iss1/8

3 The Archbishops' Antiracism Taskforce, 'Lament to Action', p. 7, accessed 28/04/2021 via www.churchofengland.org/news-and-media/news-releases/update-anti-racism-taskforce.

4 www.anglicancommunion.org/mission/marks-of-mission.aspx, accessed 28/04/2021.

5 General Synod is the legislative body of the Church of England and meets at the very least in February and July each year, but often holds a November meeting, especially for urgent legislation.

6 Church of England, 'The Five Guiding Principles', accessed 28/04/2021 via www.churchofengland.org/sites/default/files/2017-10/the_five_guiding_principles.pdf.

7 Review of Nomination to the See of Sheffield and Related Concerns: Report by the Independent Reviewer, paragraph 203, accessed 28/04/2021 via www.churchofengland.org/sites/default/files/2017-11/Review%20of%20the%20Nomination%20to%20the%20See%20of%20Sheffield%20and%20Related%20Concerns.pdf.

8 For the WATCH document see: https://womenandthechurch. org/resources/five-guiding-principles-an-introduction-and-guide/, accessed 28/04/2021; and for the Faith and Order document see: www. churchofengland.org/sites/default/files/2018-02/5%20Guiding%20 Principles.pdf, accessed 28/04/2021.

9 Forward in Faith, 'The Five Guiding Principles', accessed 28/04/2021 via www.forwardinfaith.com/WBProvisions.php?id=213.

10 Ministry Council, 'Guidance to dioceses and TEIs on support for ordinands who become parents', accessed 28/04/2021 via www. churchofengland.org/sites/default/files/2020-03/6.%20Guidance%20 note%20to%20dioceses%20and%20TEIs%20ordinands.pdf.

11 WATCH, *A Report of the Developments in Women's Ministry in 2020*, p. 10, accessed 28/04/2021 via https://womenandthechurch.org/resources/a-report-on-the-developments-in-womens-ministry-in-2020.

12 F. Gardner, *Sex, Power, Control: Responding to Abuse in the Institutional Church* (Cambridge: The Lutterworth Press, 2021), chaps 6, 9.

13 Archbishops' Council, *Setting God's People Free*, accessed 28/04/2021 via www.churchofengland.org/sites/default/files/2017-11/gs-2056-setting-gods-people-free.pdf.

Smashed

Laura Cook

Girl, go smash glass!

I have made a ladder just for you
and painted it gold
a bright and shiny thing.

Power-dress in your powder pink dress
and strap on those business heels
to make yourself tall
formidable
and start climbing
claw hammer in hand
red lipstick on mouth.

Girl, go smash glass
eyes focused on the prize
so you won't notice
that while you scale those rungs of misogyny
new steps are shaped above your head.

Paint those eyes wide
and put on your rose-tinted glasses
so you can't see
that glass ain't glass at all.
This crystal is concrete
and this ceiling comes complete with walls.

Girl. Go. Smash. Glass.
Because I told you to.
Shatter it into a thousand fragments
and
as you pick shards out of your skin
the patriarchy will raise a toast to you –
Girl with the Glittering Goals.

Misogyny and misogynoir
The afterthought.
And the thought after that.
Sarah from South London.
Blessing on a Beach in Bexhill.
And all the invisible ones
covered in a shroud
of disinformation and disinterest.
Girls that were smashing glass.

Girl.
Go smash glass.
But don't you dare raise your voice
or burn candles in the night
their light shines too brightly
and we need you climbing in the dark.

Better you focus above you
on that Sistine Chapel made of glass
than recognize the room you are in
for what it is.
A cell made of cement
A mausoleum for the missing 50 per cent.

We encourage navel gazing
breasts and buttocks too.
Focus on the skin you live within
not the systems that crush and bind you.

Girl go. Get smashed.
Then we can blame your rape
on your behaviour.
Get sequinned and hot-panted
so we can paint you as promiscuous.
Asking to be smashed up.
Begging to be glassed.

Be Bold, Fierce, Strong
Be You, Yourself, Do Your Thing.
Be Everything You Want To Be
The Just Do It generation
Just don't, don't do it
don't ask questions
notice the sneaks but not the ties
notice the watch but not the time.

Girl.
Stop.
Smashing.
Glass.

Girl stop.

Girl.
Smash systems, not ceilings.
Encourage your daughters
to construct their own castles,
build their own blueprints,
not settle for sweating
a future that is not their own.

Take liberties, curate liberty
not a cardboard cut-out of freedom
but unfiltered emancipation.
The great unshackling has begun
the Spirit moves in thin spaces
effacing and creating
places where we can all be, so

Girl go.
swallow the red pill.
become the architect
become the alchemist
become God's wildest dream.
For She never told us to go smash glass
She didn't give us a gavel of slavery
She told us to be free.

Girl go
for you were made for a time
a time such as this
crafted and constructed
in Her image beyond compare
and in Her steps you tread
without fear
for She clothes wildflowers
and She cloaks you. So go.

Girl go, be free.

Be free, girl go

7

Trans and Christian?

JACK WOODRUFF

To those who are asking – can I be trans and Christian?

The short answer is yes. The long answer will examine what the Bible says about us, what the Churches say about us and stories of those living out their trans and Christian identities side by side.

Sadly, we live in a world where people think our trans identity is somehow wrong or unnatural, and in some cases Christianity is used as a reasoning for this. As a Christian, it is hard to watch someone who claims to share in my faith in a loving God use that faith to tell us that we are wrong. As a trans person, it is hard to hear these words of hatred as I seek to find my true self in how God made me. It is especially scary when these voices shout louder than the voice of inclusivity and affirmation.

Several years ago, when I began exploring my own faith at university, I asked the same question you are asking now – can I be trans and Christian? The internet did not give me a clear answer, so I asked the first Christians I came across at university, the Christian Union. I was chatting with one of their members, Louise (not her real name), and asked if God accepts trans people. She told me that I should not challenge the way God made me and that the thoughts that I am male are some form of test or temptation. In that moment I believed her and thought 'This faith is not for me.' My trans identity was non-negotiable for me. If this 'God' did not accept me, then they were not the God for me.

However, I was not happy with the answer from Louise – the question of God's existence had not gone away. So I asked Rowan, the Anglican University Chaplain, the same question, and thankfully the answer was, 'Yes, God does love trans people and yes you can be trans and Christian.' Yet I am one of the lucky ones. And I should not feel lucky just because I discovered God loves trans people. It shouldn't even be a question we have to ask, it should be a known truth in the Church and in Christian communities, that we are loved by God and that our trans identities are not a sin. They are a living out of how God made us to be.

In hindsight, one of the problems with how Louise told me not to challenge how God made me was her assumption that God made me to be female. I do not believe this to be true. Now I can say with complete certainty that God made me trans. I don't know why, and I probably never will, but what I do know is that my trans identity is not me challenging God but a way of embracing how she made me. We are all made in the image of God whether cisgender or transgender.

We are also at a point where a new generation is growing up with a much more fluid view of gender. If the Church does not begin to recognize this, then more and more of our community are going to shy away from exploring a Christian faith. However, there are people seeking to change the Church and show that a fluid view of gender can fit within Christian teaching.

The Bible

While the notion of 'being transgender' was not around in biblical times, it is still important for us to find where our own trans narratives could run parallel to the stories in the Bible.

A lot of Christian resistance to our transgender bodies is based on the notion that we should not alter the way God made us. However, it is time we changed the narrative from transition 'changing' how God made us; rather it is *becoming* how God made us to be. It is a fulfilment of our true identity in God's image.

The first verse we are going to explore forms part of the Genesis 1 creation story. It is a familiar story that talks of the creation of light and dark (Genesis 1.3–5), the creation of land and sea (Genesis 1.9–11), as well as, among other things, trees, plants and animals (Genesis 1.11–25). On the sixth day we are told that God created humankind.

So God created humankind in his image,
in the image of God he created them;
male and female he created them. (Genesis 1.27, NRSV)

The Genesis 1 creation story has a very clear pattern of what can seem to be binaries being established. However, with more careful consideration we do not have just land or sea. Marshes exist, which are in between land and sea – in a way this forms a spectrum that goes from land to sea. Then there is the light and darkness. At the end of the day the world does not suddenly flip to dark – we have dusk and then in the morning we have dawn. These are all spectrums and not binaries so why, upon reaching the 'male and female' part, do we assume it must be a binary? Why can't the 'male and female he created them' be an expression of a spectrum of genders that exist between male and female, that are a combination of both or neither? I first encountered this idea in *Transforming: The Bible & the Lives of Transgender Christians* by Austen Harke.[1] Genesis 1.27 also tells us that humankind is created in God's image. Combined with the above reasoning, it seems clear that trans people are within this image.

We now turn to a central message of the New Testament. When asked by a lawyer what the greatest commandment is,

[Jesus] said to him, '"You shall love the Lord your God with all your heart, and with all your soul, and with all your mind." This is the greatest and first commandment. And a second is like it: "You shall love your neighbour as yourself."' (Matthew 22.36–39)

Here Jesus is asking us to love our fellow human b
selves. There are no conditions on who your neighbou
be. Regardless of who they are we are to love them, and th
people are not excluded from this.

Another verse that that is important to look at is one from
Paul's letter to the Galatians, in a section where he is outlining
the purpose of the law.

> There is no longer Jew or Greek, there is no longer slave or
> free, there is no longer male and female; for all of you are one
> in Christ Jesus. (Galatians 3.28)

This verse should not be read as a call to ignore our identities.
In this letter, Paul is addressing some of the key divisions
within society of his time, some of which still exist today, and
declaring that in Jesus these divisions can be crossed. He is
saying that our differences should not be divisions.

For Christians that should mean looking beyond whether we
are trans or not, and just accepting us for who we are and that
we are made in the image of God, just as cis people are.

Another theme that runs through the Bible is that of new
beginnings. Taking on a new name is something that many
of us do during transition and in the Bible it is written how
Saul became Paul, Sarai became Sarah, Jacob became Israel,
Abram became Abraham. While these name changes are not
made because they are transitioning, they do occur during key
moments of their lives. For example, in Genesis 17 we learn
how Sarah took on her new name:

> God said to Abraham, 'As for Sarai your wife, you shall not
> call her Sarai, but Sarah shall be her name. I will bless her,
> and moreover I will give you a son by her. I will bless her,
> and she shall give rise to nations; kings of peoples shall come
> from her.' (Genesis 17.15–16, NRSV)

The life of Jesus is another place where we can find parallels
with our own trans narratives. As Rachel Mann notes in her

book *Dazzling Darkness: Gender, Sexuality, Illness and God*, none of the four Gospels pays particular attention to Jesus' childhood.[2] The reason for this is not entirely relevant here; all that matters is that the story of Jesus is told with little reference to the first 30 years of his life. For many, but not all, of us, stories of childhood can be difficult to share, especially where telling these stories is only possible through revealing our gender assigned at birth. This leads to a silencing of our childhood stories, in a similar way that we know very little about Jesus' childhood and young adulthood.

A big part of Jesus' teaching was about rebirth into living life by the Spirit and new beginnings. I see no reason not to transition, because for me it is all about the alignment with how I and God see me and how the outside world sees me. In their book *Transgender. Christian. Human.* Alex Clare-Young notes how transformation and belonging are woven together in Christian traditions.[3] Baptism is seen as an act of transformation in which we are welcomed into the Christian community. Therefore it is in transforming ourselves to live out our calling as trans children of God that we gain a greater sense of belonging.

In the resurrection story we see a symbol of oppression, the cross, turned into a symbol of liberation through Jesus' resurrection. Prior to transition, it can feel as though our bodies, or our name, or pronouns, are oppressing us. They don't feel right, or true to ourselves. Through transitioning, in whatever form that takes for you, it is hoped that there will be a growing sense of liberation as our outward-facing selves begin to align with who we are and who God knows us to be.

With all this considered, I do not see how anyone can insist that being trans is 'unbiblical' or somehow 'against God'. We are made in the image of God just as cis people are, and never let anyone try to tell you otherwise. For those who are unsure whether their trans identity can fit in alongside a Christian identity, I hope that this has started to reassure you that it is possible to be both trans and Christian. As Alex Clare-Young points out, the writer of 1 Timothy 4 pays particular attention to identity,[4] especially in relation to a person's call to ministry being linked with their identity. From this we ascertain the importance of identity and the importance of who we are. Once again, within this notion of identity comes our own gender identity.

Transgender theology is a growing field but it still remains very small. By definition, the trans experience is different to the cis experience and this difference can be expanded to trans theology. There have been attempts to fit us into a pre-existing cis framework, which is simply not possible or true to trans experiences, hence the need for the expansion into trans theology.

Church

Having looked at what the Bible does, or does not say, about us, we shall now look at what some of the national churches say.

The Church of England

In July 2017, the Church of England General Synod (the governing body), passed The Blackburn Motion, which states:

> That this Synod, recognizing the need for transgender people to be welcomed and affirmed in their parish church, call on the House of Bishops to consider whether some nationally commended liturgical materials might be prepared to mark a person's gender transition.[5]

Following this, the House of Bishops discussed the commissioning of a specific liturgy, but decided to recommend that the existing Affirmation of Baptismal Vows service be used. Guidance was released on this, providing advice on using the existing liturgy and a clear statement of affirmation:

The Church of England welcomes and encourages the unconditional affirmation of trans people, equally with all people,
within the body of Christ, and rejoices in the diversity of that
body into which all Christians have been baptized by one
Spirit.[6]

While such a statement is a good step forward, it falls short of
what the Church of England could do if they used their power.
Beyond some guidance, we are yet to see how this statement is
going to be put into action. The hope with the commissioning
of a new liturgy was that it would show that the Church of
England recognized our unique experience as trans people and
saw that it could meet the need for trans Christians to have
the option to mark their transition within church. However,
despite the lack of commissioned liturgy from the Church of
England, liturgies that can be used to mark our gender transition have been written. These include liturgies to mark a
name change, recovery from surgery and Transgender Day of
Remembrance.[7]

The Methodist Church

In 2020 the Conference of the Methodist Church noted that
it would report in 2021 on a resolution made in 2016 and
amended in 2018. In 2020 it stated:

It rejects transphobic discrimination and calls on the Methodist people to stand with trans, intersex and non-binary
people.[8]

In 2020 the Methodist Church also released resources for
Transgender Day of Remembrance. The 2021 Conference
reaffirmed its previous resolutions.

Other Churches

From my own research I have yet to find a statement from the United Reformed Church on transgender people. In July 2019, Alex Clare-Young became the first openly transgender minister in the URC. And in the following year, after receiving significant backlash from their involvement in the Church of England *Living in Love and Faith* project, the URC released a statement in support of Alex.[9]

In 2018, the Quaker Life Central Committee released a draft statement for the consideration of Quakers in Britain, stating that '[a]s a Quaker community, we respect and uphold the self-expression of all members of and visitors to our community. We commit to using and respecting individuals' current names and pronouns.'[10] However, the draft statement has yet to be accepted.[11]

Founded in the US in 1968, Metropolitan Community Churches (MCC) was based upon the values of LGBT+ inclusion. While there was a focus on gay liberation, they have supported transgender rights for a long time. In the UK there are a few MCC communities and LGBT+ inclusion remains one of their key focuses.

The official stance of the Roman Catholic church is not an affirming one. However, there are LGBT+ Catholic spaces, and those within the church who are trying to change things. For example, there is a monthly mass held in York for the LGBT+ community. It is led by the Middlesbrough Diocese LGBT+ Ministry team.

Having looked at national church statements, it is important to note that they might not necessarily reflect the views of those in actual church congregations. In my own personal experience, I have found that individuals, and some congregations, are often more inclusive and open-minded than the national church to which they belong.

In the above cases, I have searched for examples of explicit trans inclusion. Sadly, a lot of apparently inclusive churches believe that implicit inclusion is enough. However, this does not work to undo the Church's years of prejudice and discrimination. If churches are to be inclusive spaces, for us and other oppressed groups, they need to be explicit about their welcome and inclusion. It is simply not enough to be 'not transphobic' if we are to feel welcome and valued as our whole selves.

The best way to find trans inclusive Christian spaces is to contact local LGBT+, or trans specific groups, to see if they know of inclusive churches. Or go to the Inclusive Church website and search for churches near you.[12] However, as some of us know, a space that claims to be LGBT+ inclusive is often only LGB inclusive, or even just LG inclusive. It is frustrating that we have to actively search for spaces that are safe for us to be in, in terms both of Christian communities and wider society.

It saddens me that this is something that needs to be discussed, because churches are supposed to be places that encourage the living out of Christ-like values, values which include radical inclusion and seeking justice for all.

As we are talking about how welcome we may or may not be in Christian settings, it is also worth noting that in many of the spaces we enter as openly trans people, we are often expected to be educators. The problem here is that we are then reduced to our trans identity, which, while an important part for many, isn't our entire story. The other thing is the exhaustion that comes from repeatedly having to explain something as complex as gender identity, answering inappropriate questions and challenging stereotypes, all while trying to gain a sense of belonging within that space. In response to this, the first thing to recognize is that it is not your responsibility to educate these people. There are lots of resources and books out there that you can refer people to.

However, there is a balance to be kept. Firstly, there are those who feel called to talk about their trans experiences, and these personal stories are often catalysts for change. Secondly, there is the notion of 'nothing about us without us'. If communities are trying to be more trans inclusive, then it is important that our voices are heard. This shouldn't be the responsibility of just one trans person, but nor should congregations attempt to do it alone, as this often leads to lack of genuine inclusion and affirmation. It is much better if professional facilitation is sought.

Inclusivity

My worry here, however, is that I have painted a picture that implies that we are welcome within all churches and Christian communities. The sad reality is that we are not. That is why I would like to quickly address the cisgender people who are reading this:

As a cisgender person, you have an amount of power to advocate for the inclusion of trans people. This is not to ignore other forms of discrimination; just because you are cisgender does not mean you don't have your own struggle. As a white person, I am learning about my own privilege and discerning how I can use this in the fight for racial justice, and through this learning I am able to take action. So as a cisgender person, *you can* use your privilege to challenge transphobic narratives and advocate for trans inclusion, *both* within our churches and in society as a whole.

Resources

Two of the books I have mentioned have been written by Christina Beardsley and Chris Dowd: *Transfaith: A Transgender Pastoral Resource* (2018) and *Trans Affirming Churches: How to Celebrate Gender-Variant People and Their Loved Ones* (2020). Christina Beardsley is a trans woman and Church of England priest. She is a member of The Sibyls, a Christian spirituality group for transgender people, and has been advocating for trans inclusion in the Church for many years.[13] Chris Dowd is a cis gay URC minister based in Hull who has worked with trans people for many years.

Austen Harke, whose work is also mentioned above, is

another trans Christian. He is founder and director of the Transmission Ministry Collective, an organization that provides online spaces where trans people can explore Christianity and meet other trans Christians.[14]

Alex Clare-Young, who was mentioned earlier in this chapter, is another trans Christian who is working to facilitate trans awareness both in the Church and out-with it. Their website is www.alexclareyoung.co.uk.

Conclusion

My hope here is that I have managed to show you that as well as being trans, you can also be a Christian and find Christian communities where you can be your true self. This is not so that I can convert you, that is not the aim here. It is to show those of our community who have a Christian faith, or are exploring a Christian faith, that there are places in Christianity where we are welcome. So many of our community are scared to enter any Christian space out of fear that they will be rejected because of their trans identities. We must call upon our allies to help rectify and redeem the toxic places.

For some in our community, the transphobic abuse from Christians and churches becomes a barrier to sharing in the Christian faith. The blame cannot be put on the receivers of abuse and misunderstanding. The church needs to expend energy in self-reflection, open listening, and radical restructuring to begin the process of apologizing and seeking to rebuild broken relationships with excluded members of God's world.

Notes

1 A. Harke, *Transforming: The Bible and the Lives of Transgender Christians* (Louisville, KY: Westminster John Knox Press, 2018), p. 47.

2 R. Mann, *Dazzling Darkness: Gender, Sexuality, Illness and God* (Glasgow: Wild Goose Publications, 2012).

3 A. Clare-Young, *Transgender. Christian. Human* (Glasgow: Wild Goose Publications, 2019).

4 Clare-Young, *Transgender. Christian. Human.*

5 The Church of England, 'Welcoming Transgender People' (09/07/2018), accessed 07/06/2021 via www.churchofengland.org/news-and-media/news-and-statements/welcoming-transgender-people

6 Church of England, 'Pastoral Guidance for use in conjunction with the Affirmation of Baptismal Faith in the context of gender transition', accessed 05/06/2021 via www.churchofengland.org/sites/default/files/2019-06/Pastoral%20Guidance-Affirmation-Baptismal-Faith-Context-Gender-Transition.pdf

7 C. Beardsley and C. Dowd, *Transfaith: A Transgender Pastoral Resource* (London: Darton, Longman & Todd, 2018).

8 The Methodist Conference 2020 accessed 06/07/2021 via www.methodist.org.uk/media/17862/conf-2020noticesofmotion.pdf#:~:text=The%20Conference%20of%202016%20directed%20the%20Methodist%20Council,life%20of%20the%20Church.%E2%80%99%20The%20Conference%20of%202018

9 United Reformed Church, 'URC issues statement in support of Trans minister: United in Christ through God's calling' (02/12/2020) accessed 12/06/2021 via www.agilitypr.news/URC-issues-statement-in-support-of-Trans-13940

10 Quaker Life Central Committee 'Quakers and Gender Diversity: Discussion Document' (November 2018) accessed 12/06/2021 via https://quaker-prod.s3.eu-west-1.amazonaws.com/store/0b13f483a23ed380b4c963c9561b0fa281d1a9de63b4271f1061625a8ac2

11 Quaker Gender and Sexual Diversity Community, 'Quakers and Transgender People', accessed 13/06/2021 via https://qgsdc.org.uk/workingforequality/quakers-and-transgender-people/

12 Inclusive Church, accessed 13/06/2021 via www.inclusive-church.org/.

13 The Sibyls, accessed 14/06/2021 via http://sibyls.gndr.org.uk/

14 Transmission Ministry Collective, accessed 14/06/2021 via www.transmissionministry.com

8

Waking Up to Ableism in Christian Communities

CHRISSIE THWAITES

Introduction

Approximately one billion people globally experience some type of disability.[1] Disability is widespread, but it is not new, nor does it specifically pertain to young people. The term 'woke', meanwhile, has emerged only in the last century, entering the UK vernacular in the past decade. So why include a chapter on disability in this book? What has disability to do with wokeness? In short, though disability activism has made great gains in the past half-century, it still has a long way to go. Through this chapter I hope to re-energise conversations about disability in churches and shine a light on ableism.

In recent decades legislation has solidified legal protection for people with disabilities, but this has not yet generated equality.[2] Disabled people continue to be at a higher risk of poverty,[3] and a report on disability inequality showed that 'in many sectors we have failed to make real progress, and in some areas we have even gone backwards'.[4] There is a growing awareness of this inequality, and conversations about disability have also been revitalized as awareness of hidden disabilities has increased. In the UK, one in five people have a disability, and 80 per cent of these people have a hidden disability.[5] These may not be immediately apparent and include, for example, sensory impairments, autism spectrum disorder, ADHD, dyslexia and dyspraxia, mental illness and chronic illnesses (such as Crohn's disease, arthritis, cystic fibrosis, chronic fatigue syndrome and Alzheimer's).[6] A growing acknowledgement of these varied experiences of disability has brought well-needed attention to lived realities that have long gone unnoticed. There are motivated young people at the forefront of this shift. And they are in our churches.

Understanding disability

Disability studies is a relatively young field, emerging from the disability rights movement of the 1960s and 70s, and initially focused on critiquing existing conceptions of disability. A new social model of disability was formulated, distinguished from the previously dominant medical model, and was widely accepted by the 1990s. Two important points arose from these conversations: (1) the role of social barriers in disability, and (2) the significance of impairment.

The social model of disability

The social model sees the cause of disability as barriers from society. It rejects the medical model, which understands disability as a problem or defect located in the individual, and instead sees disability as a socially constructed phenomenon.[7] Within the social model, impairment is distinguished from disability: impairment (such as blindness, deafness, lack of mobility) is 'individual and private', while disability is 'structural and public'.[8] The expectation of change is thus relocated from the individual to the built environments social conditions, attitudes and assumptions that are disabling. Disability is not something one has, but 'the product of malignant social practices'.[9] The social model therefore calls into question the organization of society around able-bodiedness and assumptions of what is 'normal'.

Impairment

The social model has received scrutiny for devaluing some of the challenges of impairment, especially in relation to pain, discomfort and the emotional impact of a changing body.[10] Systematic theologian Deborah Creamer has critiqued the social model on this basis, arguing that it does not leave space for the complexity of people's relationships with their impairment (which could be negative or ambivalent).[11] Though pain and/or discomfort is 'a dimension of the oppressive quality of chronic illness and disability for large numbers of people', the dominance of the social models means that such aspects of living with impairments can go under-acknowledged.[12]

This is not to say that the social model should be dismantled, just that it does not have all-encompassing descriptive power for experiences of disability. The originators of this model have themselves noted that it was an attempt not 'to deal with the personal restrictions of impairment' but rather to address 'the social barriers of disability'.[13] Disabling social structures need to be acknowledged alongside the (often challenging) realities of impairment. This is a helpful message for the Church to take on board.

Creating a disability-woke Church: moving from inclusion to justice

Many churches and Christian networks in the UK have committed to making their communities both physically accessible and socially inclusive. This commitment to disability inclusion is reflected at an institutional level in my own denomination, the Church of England, by the Committee for the Ministry of and among Deaf and Disabled People.[14] Indeed, my own experiences have often shown me that churches are keen to ensure disabled people are valued, involved and loved members of their congregations. But disability is not just an issue of inclusion; it is also one of justice. And this is where the Church falls short.

Disability and justice

What makes disability an issue of justice? Legal protection for the rights of disabled people has not yet translated into equality in practice. For example, the relationship between disability and poverty is startling; 31 per cent of people with disabilities in the UK live in poverty, compared to a poverty rate of 20 per cent among the rest of the population, and half of all people in poverty either 'have a disability themselves or live with someone who does'.[15] Sixty-two per cent of working-age adults referred to food banks are disabled.[16] The EHRC report on disability inequality emphasized: lack of access to mental health care and appropriate health services, inadequacy of housing and transport, an increasingly persistent disability pay gap, lower educational attainment rates for students with disabilities, deteriorating access to justice, and welfare reforms that disproportionately affect disabled people.[17]

In 2016, the UK became the first signatory state to be investigated over human rights breaches by the UN Convention on the Rights of Persons with Disabilities. The resulting UN report concluded that 'grave or systematic violations' of this convention had taken place, particularly through reforms to the welfare system since 2010 which had 'adverse and disproportionate effects' on people with disabilities.[18] Key areas of concern included changes to Housing Benefit entitlement, the introduction of Personal Independence Payment, and an ongoing policy of reducing social benefits. Risk of material deprivation and rampant inequality are only compounded by social attitudes that see people with disabilities as less valuable members of society. Myths about disability, such as the 'skiver vs striver' narrative (perpetuated by the media and hidden in the ideologies driving cuts to state welfare), only further reveal the state of disability inequality and discrimination in the UK.

The concept of disability justice understands disability and ableism in the context of other forms of discrimination, and it is helpful to note here. It is thus distinct from (though related to) the idea of disability as a justice issue, and focuses on how ableism interacts with other forms of oppression. Disability justice therefore ensures that disabled people are not homogenised; it encourages activism that acknowledges that disability is not a universally identical experience and rallies behind those most at risk of oppression, discrimination and disadvantage because of their overlapping social identities. Taking this approach in church communities helps us to ensure that our pursuit of justice is informed by, and resonates with, lived experiences.

The politicization of justice: a barrier to Christian action?

In my experience, when justice becomes politicized the Church often loses interest. But disabled people and their loved ones are exposed to discrimination, misunderstanding and inequality, so this is often the precise point at which we need the Church to be our ally. Many of these experiences arise from policies implemented by governments, such as those relating to welfare support, employment or discrimination; it is often the case that the lived reality of disability cannot be divorced from politics.

This may seem distinct from the call of the Church. But throughout the Bible we see God's express concern for the social conditions of humanity. The Hebrew Bible reveals God's commands for just and righteous living among his people; Israel is to be a land of justice (e.g. Deuteronomy 16.20; Deuteronomy 24.17; Exodus 23.1–9; Isaiah 1.26–17; Micah 6.8; Zechariah 7.9–11). Some people consider social justice a societal trend or fad. But the biblical mandate to justice is not. Biblical justice is grounded in God's unchanging character, of which justice is a central part (Psalms 10.14–18; 33.5; 37.28; 89.14; 99.4; 103.6; 111.7–8). As Chris Marshall puts it, 'our knowledge of justice springs ultimately from our knowledge of God', and the Christian life therefore entails 'both an appreciation of God's own unswerving devotion to justice and a commitment to live one's personal life in conformity to God's justice'.[19] We profess our knowledge and love of God and others through our actions, and by living distinctively in 'relationships that uphold the equal dignity and rights of the other'.[20]

If the Church is to manifest the kingdom of God, emulate the love of Jesus, restore dignity and reverse the unequal power dynamics and self-righteous attitudes that engender inequality, it cannot shy away from the pursuit of justice – including the ways in which this can entail politically and socially engaged action. Indeed, Jesus' proclamation of the kingdom of God stood in opposition to unjust social orders that involved exclusion, exploitation and unequal distribution of resources and power. We cannot be committed to disability inclusion and equality without also being committed to eradicating the causes of exclusion and inequality.

Becoming an enabling church

What can churches do to become enabling rather than disabling? How can they move beyond disability inclusion to justice? Outlined here are some harmful practices to move away from, and suggested practices to move towards.

Address ableist legacies, practices and theologies

In his book *I Am Strong*, Lamar Hardwick considers Jesus' parable of the lost sheep. Interpretations of this parable often focus on the lone sheep who has gone astray: 'For years, I assumed that the primary point of this story is the sinfulness of the missing sheep', Hardwick shares.[21] But, he wonders, what if the sheep is not the one at fault? 'What if the greatest lesson to be learned is not the sinfulness of the sheep, but rather the shamefulness of a community that sees itself as complete while one of its own is missing?'[22]

I invite you to consider the ways in which your flock may have allowed sheep to become isolated, and how it may have seen itself as complete despite some of its own being missing.

Think of how many worship songs equate impairment with sin and spiritual failure, or of the times people with disabilities have been told God could cure them if only they had enough faith. Think of the theological justifications used for ableism (seeing disability as punishment, the result of sin). Consider too how Christian theology has bought into a capitalist work ethic that measures value as economic productivity, or the long history of physically inaccessible church buildings. All of these contribute to an ableist culture in which there is no place for disabled people. Creating churches that are inclusive of people with disabilities goes beyond inclusion initiatives. It demands active reflection on ableist legacies, theologies and practices.

Reconsider 'curing' language

Many disabled people know all too well the experience of unsolicited prayers. For some, the offer of prayer – and the associated fellowship, mutuality and well-meaning sentiments – can be comforting. But in many cases, these prayers represent an unwelcome suggestion that there is something wrong that needs fixing. Using language that casts disabled people in the role of the victim creates a world in which disability diverges from what is 'normal' and perpetuates ableism by constructing disability as inferior.

The miracles of Jesus are sometimes employed as a foundation for curing prayers, but it is important to note the *holistic healing* present in these narratives. Healing and curing are not the same thing; curing has to do with fixing and mending, healing has to do with (re)connection. Jesus did not simply cure impairments; he restored social status, welcomed the marginalized, and engaged freely with people stigmatized *because* of their impairment. Appealing to potential cures can be problematic because it implies a return to former abilities or bodily faculties (which in many cases is not possible and for some was never a reality), and homogenizes the diverse experiences of disability. Sometimes, there may be an easily observable cure, for example from a temporary impairment that is the result of an injury. For others, disability and impairment are permanent and bound up with one's embodied identity. Theologian Frances Young, reflecting on her son Arthur who has intellectual disabilities, says that 'healed he would be a different person'.[23]

Cultivate communities without judgement

In church communities, I have found, it is very easy to settle into a status quo. Whether this is the order of services, how the building is laid out, the times at which events take place, how furniture is arranged, how resources are stored, you name it – it is common to remain set in a particular (familiar) way of doing things. The problem with this is that some people cannot conform to these patterns, and judgement flows easily. This is true for people with disabilities, especially hidden disabilities. These are not immediately obvious and as such peoples' needs might not be anticipated or could be misunderstood. Possible assumptions and questions include 'Why are you sitting there?', 'Why are you using that disabled parking space?', 'Why are you leaving in the middle of a service?' Perhaps, for people with mobility issues, arthritis or chronic fatigue, it's 'Why aren't you joining in?' For autistic people, the need to mask in order to avoid judgement or hurt can be profound, at risk of being exposed to facial expressions which betray 'Why are you being like that?' Judgement for non-compliance doesn't help people feel like they are included.

Commit to presence and dwell in limits

While we dismantle these structures, informed by the social model of disability, we must also consider the realities of discomfort and pain that impairment can bring. In my experience, Christian communities can struggle to sit with pain and lived realities which challenge existing worldviews. We are not used to dwelling in discomfort, striving instead to 'fix' things and reassert control over the unpredictability of life. What if we replaced this impulse with a commitment to presence among uncertainty and difference? What if we committed in equal measure to deconstructing the disabling social barriers we have put up *and* to showing up when the reality of impairment means people need support?

Further to this, inequalities arising from both social disabilities and the realities of impairment mean that often activism is needed. Are we going to be active agents present *within* this cause, or just well-meaning witnesses to it? Are you going to pursue justice for disabled people in how you engage in your local area, how you spend your energy/money/time, how you vote? Being fully present means sharing in each other's lived realities, living in equitable community, and taking action when the cultures, attitudes, economies and politics of our societies bring about inequality.

The call to presence reflects the reality of limitedness as a conventional part of human existence and compels us to dwell in our shared vulnerability. Such a way of life would enact what theologian Deborah Creamer describes as a 'theology of limits', which frames disability as an 'unsurprising aspect of being human'.[24] It dismantles the binary of normality vs deviance which is often employed to make sense of disability. Disability is a normal state of embodied existence, and is an (immensely broad) category open to anyone.[25] To be limited is not to have failed, or to have missed the mark of full humanness or perfection; to be limited is simply to be human. Theologian Tom Reynolds notes that humans are naturally dependent on one another and have a shared vulnerability,[26] mirrored in God who partakes in humanity's vulnerability through the Incarnation.[27] Conceptions of human perfection that utilize the *imago Dei* often exclude disability, but, as John Swinton notes, the image of God 'cannot be claimed by any group of human beings'; 'human variation doesn't have any specifically theological or moral significance', humans are 'simply varied and loved'.[28] The call to presence compels us to reside in this limitedness together, whatever it may look like.

Engagement and representation

Discussions of disability inclusion and justice are meaningless without the voices of disabled people, so it is important to include these voices in constructive dialogue. Has your church done enough? Have previous inclusion efforts worked? How and why do people continue to feel excluded? It is easy to talk about inclusion and belonging in the abstract, but are practical questions seriously considered? For example, is your church building physically accessible for people who have reduced mobility? Does the structure of your service privilege specific ways of being and exclude people with ASD/ADHD? Are there unspoken assumptions about how people experience God that can be exclusionary? Are toilets accessible, and is access discreet enough that use of them isn't brought to everyone's attention? Why not incorporate British Sign Language into your services (if you already encourage actions with songs or prayers, this could be an easy step)? Does the kind of sound you produce work well in a hearing loop or for those who have hearing aids? You will find the answers to these sorts of questions by listening to disabled people in your community. A church's approach to disability is best shaped by and with people with disabilities. As noted above, this may get political – don't shy away from this. If justice for people with disabilities involves addressing the widespread disability inequality in your community, your region, your nation, you have no option but to engage. Expanding inclusion initiatives and embracing disabled people as participant members of your community will naturally extend to involvement with disability justice.

As well as engaging with disabled voices, it is important also to ensure disabled people are present at all levels of the church, and represented in leadership in a way that reflects the make-up of the congregation. Are people with disabilities equally encouraged to enter ministry and adequately supported during the discernment process? In a recent *Church Times* article, Naomi Lawson Jacobs noted that disabled people are often positioned by their churches 'as recipients of others' service rather than as co-creators of the Kingdom of God', and that 'ministries for disabled people by well-meaning non-disabled people rather than ministries by and with disabled people are often the norm'.[29] It's time to change this, to recognize the gifts and skills of disabled people, and to distribute roles and responsibilities that reflect these.

Celebration, not (just) lamentation

This idea – that disabled people are not simply people to be taken care of but have much to contribute – reminds us to celebrate, encourage and recognize the many ways in which disabled people are valuable. Too often the emphasis is on how communities should adapt to include people, rather than how those people can contribute to the community. The late blind theologian John M. Hull summarized this well:

> Disabled people are not so much a pastoral problem as a prophetic potential. We need to ask not how the church can care for disabled people but to ask what is the prophetic message of the church in our culture and how disabled people can make a unique contribution to that renewal … My question is not what we have to learn from disabled people but how the whole church can respond to its evangelical calling and how disabled people can not only participate in this but can become witnesses to and leaders of it.[30]

What if the question was not simply 'How can we be inclusive?' but 'How do this person's skills, talents, opinions and unique life experiences bless this community and beyond?'. The Church has an opportunity to be a prophetic voice to the world, to set precedent beyond its own walls for celebrating *all* people and dismantling unhelpful assumptions that see disabled people as charity cases solely to be cared for.

Conclusion

This chapter constitutes an effort to bring disability to the forefront of conversations about justice and inclusion in church communities. I have provided an overview of the social theory of disability, considered obstacles to creating a disability-woke church, identified disability as a justice issue and offered suggestions on how to make churches enabling rather than disabling.

It also attempts to replicate the urgency and passion that other areas of justice have received in recent years. Young people are particularly aware of the need for change and are raising their voices in disability activism. While the term 'woke' is often weaponized to disparagingly identify such young people, in reality we are not interested in divisive identity politics, virtue signalling or self-righteousness. Rather, we are awake to inequality and committed to pursuing justice. We may get things wrong along the way but we are here, ready to do the work of creating a disability-woke Church. We hope you will join us.

Notes

1 World Bank, *Disability Inclusion* (2021), accessed 08/04/2021 via www.worldbank.org/en/topic/disability.

2 Disability Discrimination Act (1995); Equality Act (2010).

3 Joseph Rowntree Foundation, *UK Poverty 2020/21: The leading independent report* (2021), pp. 16–17, accessed 20/05/2021 via www.jrf.org.uk/report/uk-poverty-2020-21

4 Equality and Human Rights Commission (EHRC), *Being Disabled in Britain: A journey less equal* (2017), p. 5, accessed 20/08/2021 via www.equalityhumanrights.com/sites/default/files/being-disabled-in-britain.pdf

5 Hidden Disabilities, *What is a hidden disability?* (2021), accessed 08/04/2021 via hiddendisabilitiesstore.com/what-is-a-hidden-disability

6 Not everyone who experiences these will identify as disabled. Disability is an enormously broad category, and I include these examples not to impose labels which some may not identify with, but to acknowledge experiences that are often ignored or forgotten.

7 G. Williams, 'Theorizing Disability', in G. L. Albrecht, K. Seelman and M. Bury, eds, *Handbook of Disability Studies* (Thousand Oaks, CA: SAGE Publications, 2001), pp. 123–44, p. 136.

8 T. Shakespeare, 'The Social Model of Disability', in L. J. Davis, ed., *The Disability Studies Reader, 5th edition* (New York: Routledge, 2017), pp. 195–203, p. 197.

9 J. Swinton, 'Who is the God we worship? Theologies of disability; challenges and new possibilities', *International Journal of Practical Theology* (Vol.14, 2011), pp. 273–307, pp. 280–1.

10 M. Oliver, 'Defining Impairment and Disability: Issues at Stake', in E. F. Emens and S. B. Goldberg, eds, *Disability and Equality Law* (New York: Routledge, 2013), pp. 3–89, pp. 11–12.

11 D. Creamer, *Disability and Christian Theology* (New York: Oxford University Press, 2009), p. 27.

12 Williams, 'Theorizing Disability', p. 135.

13 Oliver, 'Defining Impairment', p. 12.

14 Church of England, *Welcoming Disabled People*, accessed 08/04/2021 via www.churchofengland.org/resources/welcoming-disabled-people

15 Joseph Rowntree Foundation, *UK Poverty 2019/20: The leading independent report* (2021), p. 8, p. 21, accessed 20/05/2021 via www.jrf.org.uk/report/uk-poverty-2019-20

16 Trussell Trust, *State of Hunger: Year Two Main Report* (2021), p. 25, accessed 12/08/2021 via www.trusselltrust.org/wp-content/uploads/sites/2/2021/05/State-of-Hunger-2021-Report-Final.pdf

17 EHRC, *Being Disabled in Britain*, p. 7.

18 UN Committee on the Rights of Persons with Disabilities, *Inquiry concerning the United Kingdom of Great Britain and Northern Ireland carried out by the Committee under article 6 of the Optional Protocol to the Convention* (2016), p. 20, accessed 20/05/2021 via www.ohchr.org/Documents/HRBodies/CRPD/CRPD.C.15.R.2.Rev.1-ENG.doc; cf. House of Commons, *Briefing paper: The UN Convention on the Rights of Persons with Disabilities: UK implementation* (2020), p. 4, accessed 20/05/2021 via https://researchbriefings.files.parliament.uk/documents/CBP-7367/CBP-7367.pdf

19 C. Marshall, *The Little Book of Biblical Justice* (Intercourse, PA: Good Books, 2005), p. 25, p. 27.

20 Marshall, *Biblical Justice*, p. 36.

21 L. Hardwick, *I Am Strong: The life and journey of an autistic pastor* (Little Elm, TX: eLectio Publishing, 2017), p. 10.

22 Hardwick, *I Am Strong*, p. 11.

23 F. Young, *Face to Face: A narrative essay in the theology of suffering* (Edinburgh: T&T Clark, 1990), p. 22.

24 Creamer, *Disability and Christian Theology*, p. 93.

25 Creamer, *Disability and Christian Theology*, p. 32.

26 T. E. Reynolds, *Vulnerable Communion: A Theology of Disability and Hospitality* (Grand Rapids, MI: Baker Publishing Group, 2008), p. 84.

27 Reynolds, *Vulnerable Communion*, p. 223.

28 Swinton, 'Who is the God we worship?', p. 301.

29 N. Lawson Jacobs, 'Disabled people say welcome to our world', *Church Times*, (2020), accessed 20/05/2021 via: www.churchtimes.co.uk/articles/2020/1-may/features/features/disabled-people-say-welcome-to-our-world I highly recommend Lawson Jacobs' work. She also offers Disability Equality Training for churches. See: http://naomilawsonjacobs.com/.

30 J. M. Hull and B. Callaghan, *Disability: The Inclusive Church Resource* (London: Darton, Longman and Todd, 2014), p. 60.

9

Food Poverty:
Bread of Life? Or Bread for Life?

ANNA TWOMLOW

> Therefore I tell you, do not worry about your life, what you
> will eat or drink; or about your body, what you will wear.
> Is not life more than food, and the body more than clothes?
> Look at the birds of the air; they do not sow or reap or store
> away in barns, and yet your heavenly Father feeds them. Are
> you not much more valuable than they? Can any one of you
> by worrying add a single hour to your life? (Matthew 6.25–
> 27)

'I tell you, do not worry about your life, what you will eat and
drink.'

That's easy when you are fed, clothed and watered. Less
easy if you don't know where your next meal will come from.

Despite there being more than enough food on the planet
to feed everyone, it is estimated that 8 per cent of the world's
population went to bed hungry every night in 2019.[1] That's
690 million hungry people who did not know where, when or
what they were going to next eat.

Some conservative theology tells us that true life comes from
faith in Jesus. And that true life is more important than food,
water or clothing. This theology teaches people to turn away
from materialism, and to fear consumerism because it will
become a stumbling block to their faith. They interpret Jesus'
teaching that the poor will always be 'with us'[2] (or 'beside us')

to mean that suffering will always exist because it is necessary to keep us humble and close to God. They teach that the poor have the greatest need for God because of their lack of material well-being, and that anything we give to them materially should lead them to faith in Christ because they see Jesus in the giver.

But is physical food, for a physical body, not necessary to simply be alive in our physical world? Is being alive not a necessary precursor to having faith? To being human?

Other conservative theology teaches that not worrying requires full dependence on God; surrender your worries to God and God will reward you because God is good. The idea that worrying is a sign of lacklustre faith has become pervasive in circles that follow this theology. Those who worry are told to pray harder, to be convicted of their lack of devotion to a God who is always good.

However, I totally disagree with these interpretations.

I don't think that Jesus was teaching us that worrying is shameful, or that poverty is inevitable and required for faith. Jesus told us not to worry, because we should always be able to depend on our brothers and sisters, our community, for our material needs. There will always be enough food, water and clothing provided by God within creation – so long as we justly share it. But perhaps Jesus knew that we would never share justly, and therefore 'the poor' would always exist. Perhaps he was using the term 'poor' in a more metaphorical, spiritual sense. Or maybe he was a human, speaking to his friends, highlighting that in their lifetime, poverty would always exist. Either way, we know that the early Church that those disciples and friends went on to found was a place of shared material wealth where everyone's needs were met.[3] They were a group of people who took God's charge that 'There will be no one in need among you' very seriously (Deuteronomy 15.4).

John Wesley, the (reluctant) founder of Methodism (and lifetime Anglican), also took this charge seriously. He dedicated his life to the poor and regularly begged on their behalf. Estimates suggest that during his lifetime he gave away roughly US$6 million (just over £4 million) in modern terms to the poor, and died with only US$2000 (just under £1,500) to his name.[4]

In 1738, Wesley purchased 'The Foundery', which became the centre for his mission and his followers, providing food, clothing, shelter, medical care and even financial support in the form of small loans to London's poor. It is out of these social justice roots that the Methodist mission grew. Wesley preached that the ability to give is a gift from God in and of itself. He taught Methodists that we should earn all we can and save all we can, so that we are able to give all we can. He preached that material blessings are never solely for one's own enjoyment, but are also for the benefit of the poor and the bringing about of God's Kingdom – a kingdom of justice, joy and peace. Theology that teaches a fear of materialism should actually teach the fear of wanting in excess, not in wanting sufficiency.

As a Methodist, each year I pray the covenant prayer. I pray that God will

> Put me to what you will, rank me with whom you will; put me to doing, put me to suffering; let me be employed for you, or laid aside for you, exalted for you, or brought low for you … I freely and wholeheartedly yield all things to your pleasure and disposal.

This prayer underpins my faith as a Methodist. It highlights my understanding that as a Christian I am an active participant in Christ's mission of loving a gracious God with all my heart, mind and soul and loving my neighbour as I love myself.

The prayer reminds me of Christ's self-giving, and self-emptying love and challenges me to live my life in that same way. Sometimes, loving my neighbours as I love myself requires trusting God far more than I trust myself – trusting God when I am exalted and employed and also when I am brought low and suffering. Within this prayer, suffering is understood to mean the opposite of doing – as patiently enduring nothingness and depending on others for sustenance.[5] Maybe 'suffering' refers to overcoming our human instincts of independence and pride in order to humble ourselves and recognize our need to depend on God and each other for our material and spiritual well-being.

Nearly 300 years after Wesley began 'The Foundery', the poor are still with us. If Jesus did indeed mean that the reason we needn't worry about what we will eat or drink is that we will always be able to depend on each other for our material needs, we have failed miserably. Poverty and hunger have been steadily increasing worldwide over the last decade. Nearly one quarter of all human beings are now affected by moderate or severe food insecurity.[6] The number of people experiencing this kind of food insecurity is estimated to have grown by 83–132 million during the COVID-19 pandemic.[7] In the UK, it is estimated that between 8 and 10 per cent of all households, about 8.4 million people, struggle to afford to eat.[8] Even before the pandemic, around 2.5 per cent of all households regularly used food banks every year, with use increasing nearly 17 per cent between 2016–2020.[9]

These statistics are an embarrassment to all of us who have enough.

And they are more than statistics. They are the stories of millions of people's lives, who have been condemned to a life of deficiency by us, their fellow human beings.

Our God is compassionate

Our God is compassionate. And as a result of this compassion, the Church has historically engaged in food poverty on a needs basis, addressing the symptoms of food poverty through missions, night shelters and food banks. As Christians, our giving should be rooted in gratitude for God's generosity, as a way to share all that we have. And if we are able to not worry about what we will eat or drink tomorrow, we should also want the same for our neighbours – that they will easily have access to food again tomorrow. However, even if all of us, together as the Church worldwide, earned all we can and saved all we can, so that we were able to give all we can, in the hope that everyone would have enough, this would provide only temporary relief.

Food poverty is a systemic injustice in itself, in that it is a symptom of so many wider structural and systemic injustices and immoralities. Race, gender, class, disability and socio-economic inequalities all exacerbate food poverty. Providing food to the hungry is a quick-fix to the symptoms of a much bigger problem. It is not a long-term compassionate solution. The Church should be addressing the causes of food poverty as well as it's symptoms. By addressing food poverty's causes, the Church could expose the deepest fault lines that run through our global society.

However, these are the very same fault lines that the main-stream Church (the 'capital C Church') itself has helped, inadvertently or purposefully, to create and uphold in the Western world. For example, the Church has historically played a role in creating and upholding social gender inequal-ities through harmful, patriarchal, traditional and cultural teaching.[10] The Church also played a role in colonialism and the transatlantic slave trade, which has resulted in the long-term subjugation and oppression of people of colour.[11] Additionally, the Church has historically marginalized people with disabilities, by making disability a problem through its teachings and excluding them through its rules.[12]

Of course, the wider Church has also had a role in dis-mantling these same injustices – for example by campaigning for the abolition of the slave trade, and through the develop-ment of feminist and liberation theologies. But these liberal movements tend to be born outside the 'capital C' Church. These movements and ideas that oppose oppression tend to take shape on the fringe and slowly move towards the main-stream as they become more widely embraced. Once these movements go mainstream and are backed by the power of the Church, they receive the attention and drive needed to create widespread change.

This ability for the Church to create widespread change holds a lot of potential. If harnessed, the mainstream Church could bring about a deep revolution towards justice by addressing the role that race, gender, class, disability and socioeconomic inequalities all play in exacerbating food poverty. The Church would need to listen to those who are marginalized both inside its walls and outside, and understand how all of these different inequalities interact to create food injustice. These inequalities are deeply entrenched within the structures of our society, which is why poverty seems an insurmountable problem. But if we are called to help our neighbours not to worry what they will eat and drink tomorrow, we are called to help dismantle these structures and ensure our neighbours will have access to food.

Within the development and aid sectors, there has been a significant shift in a similar vein: from short-term relief to longer-term interventions. For example, in the last decade the humanitarian organization UN World Food Program (WFP) has shifted from food aid to food assistance; the organization has moved from being a provider of food to being a provider of broader hunger solutions.[13] This is due to a paradigm shift about the way in which we understand causes of hunger. Hunger is no longer understood as temporary and anomalous due to environmental or political upheavals, but rather as a failure of entire food and agricultural systems.[14] Conflict, the climate crisis and extreme weather events drive short-term hunger because food systems are not well-equipped to deal with these disruptions. Gender and economic and social inequality drive longer-term hunger by creating barriers that prevent certain groups of people from having regular access to nutritious food.

By focusing on the drivers of hunger and the ways in which structures within food systems interact to create barriers, WFP has been able to provide food assistance that can be leveraged to make food systems more resilient. They have researched how gender, socioeconomic status and access to social protection (the range of policies and programmes needed to reduce the lifelong consequences of poverty and exclusion) impede or improve people's ability to function and access food within a given food system.[15]

In the UK, the COVID-19 crisis has exposed just how fragile our food system is, and how vulnerable those within the system are. The number of people living from one payday to another was revealed, when during the first month of lockdown in 2020, food banks saw an 89 per cent increase in their use.[16] This included a 107 per cent increase in the number of food parcels given to children, compared to the same period in 2019.[17] These people were tipped into crisis because the food system and its accompanying social protection policies did not function well enough to keep the newly unemployed, recently bereaved and mentally ill afloat. By August 2020, 28 per cent of people experienced a decrease in income due to either job losses, pay or hours cuts, or being furloughed, and in January 2021 over a fifth of people in the UK still had less monthly income than in January 2020.[18]

When formal support systems such as advice services or debt management agencies were shut down due to lockdowns, and informal support networks such as family, friends and civil society were disrupted due to quarantining, over 2.5 million people were forced to turn to food banks to meet their immediate needs.[19] Of these 2.5 million people, 9 per cent identified as Black British, which is three times higher than would be expected if the numbers were representative of the wider population, and now Black and minoritized ethnic adults in the UK are twice as likely to experience food insecurity as White British adults.[20] This is an example of how racial inequalities exacerbate food poverty. The same is true of people who experience health problems and disabilities: at the start of the pandemic, adults who identify as being limited a lot by health problems or a disability were three times more likely to be food insecure than those without, but these inequalities have increased even further and, in January 2021, they were five times higher.[21]

The Church needs to campaign against these systemic inequalities, both locally and worldwide, in order to play a role in bringing about food justice. The Church cannot simply provide food to the hungry, but should be working alongside charities and organizations to ensure that the most vulnerable people within food systems are not left behind. It needs to be involved in creating more resilient food and reducing economic inequality. The Church should speak loudly to name and criticize the drivers of short-term hunger and the inequalities that exacerbate long-term food poverty, and should fight the systems that uphold these inequalities. That is the beginning of a justice revolution. That is true compassion.

Our God is just

Our God is just.

But this doesn't mean that God is a judge. Our God is not one who is interested in morally judging us as good or bad, as some would have you believe. Divine grace has already taken care of that.

Our God's heart is rooted in justice. That is why our God is just.

God's love is rooted in equity and equality for all people. The God who railed against the injustice experienced by Israelite slaves over 6000 years ago is the same God who rails against food poverty today.

That's why the Church should be interested in a justice revolution. The Church should be taking action towards food justice – action that is placed within a system that is so complex that such actions are intrinsically linked with other forms of justice. We cannot seek to provide food for everyone today and tomorrow without addressing the inequalities about which I have already spoken.

These inequalities are rooted in our histories; histories based on the idea that wealth is deserved because of hard work and blessings from God. And that poverty is merely a symptom of laziness. This framework enforces the idea that if you do not work hard enough someone else will gain more than you.

In essence, they will gain your share, because they deserve it. Within this framework, when the rich give to the poor, it is so that they might practice humility and experience something of God through their giving. The rich do not give to the poor in order to change the fate of the poor. They do not give so that the poor might improve their lot in life, their overall well-being. The rich give, while also hoping to maintain the status quo.

Within the international development and aid sector, the shift to food assistance referred to earlier has resulted in some organizations piloting unconditional cash transfers.[22] An unconditional cash transfer is a direct transfer of money to a person with 'no strings attached' – there are no preconditions a person must meet in order to receive the money, or specific actions that a person must carry out with the money.[23] Unconditional cash transfers allow those in need to decide what they need most, whether it is food, shelter, medicine or something else. Recipients are provided with flexibility when they receive an unconditional cash transfer, and are able to make their own decisions about how to provide for their future, not just their today. Unconditional cash transfers have been shown to improve long-term living standards, increase disposable income and provide higher levels of psychological well-being and food security.[24]

Throughout 2020 and 2021, the UK government has been criticized for the distribution of free school meals. The government contracted companies to send meal packages to children's homes in England, rather than provide cash or supermarket vouchers as was the norm in Wales and Scotland.[25] However, the packages that were sent out were inadequate, because the private companies wanted to maximize profits, so they spent as little as possible on the food packages.[26] As a result, eventually the government expanded vouchers and cash to England too. At that point though, children had already gone to bed hungry and parents had already given up their own meals so that they could afford to feed their children. Furthermore, even these cash and voucher transfers were widely criticized as insufficient due to the criteria that beneficiaries needed to fulfil to receive them.[27]

Given that the evidence points towards the success of unconditional cash transfers in reducing hunger and food poverty, it is surprising that the UK government is reluctant to promote their use. Indeed, worldwide, governments and organizations are hesitant to roll out these programmes on a large scale, for example through universal basic income. Those with power and money are willing to give the poor enough to survive, but not to thrive, because that maintains the status quo.

The Church should want to change this framework and status quo. It should be supporting politics and organizations that disrupt the idea that the rich decide what the poor need. Withholding choice and autonomy is inherently un-Christian, because God has gifted us ultimate free-will and autonomy. Jesus wanted to change the fate of the poor and the hungry, and the Church should want that too.

Our God is materialistic

Our God is materialistic.

In that God is undeniably concerned with having everyone's materialistic needs met. Otherwise, Jesus would have never told us not to worry about what we shall eat or drink.

It is up to us to help people not to worry. To earn all we can and to save all we can, so we can give all we can. And to change the framework of the world in which we do that giving, to bring about justice as called for by those most affected by injustices. As a Methodist, justice for the poor runs in my blood. As Christians, it should fire our souls.

If the Church does not challenge the very systems that keep vulnerable people entrenched in poverty, and the inadequate solutions that are currently provided to those systems, the Church is a hypocrite.

The Church should not be satisfied at food for today – but rather ridding the world of hunger entirely.

Notes

1 United Nations Department of Economic and Social Affairs (2021), 'Goal 2 | Department of Economic and Social Affairs', accessed 23/06/2021 via https://sdgs.un.org/goals/goal2.

2 John 12.8, Matthew 26.13.

3 Acts 2.42–47; 4.32–34; L. V. Toews (2019), 'Motivation for the Sharing of Material Possessions in Acts, Philo's De Vita Contemplativa and the Didache: A Comparative Study', PhD dissertation, https://digitalcommons.andrews.edu/dissertations/1692.

4 M. Mann, 'John Wesley on Homelessness and Poverty' (2011), accessed 23/06/2021 via https://viewpoint.pointloma.edu/john-wesley-on-homelessness-and-poverty/.

5 The Methodist Church of Great Britain (2021), 'A covenant with God', accessed 23/06/2021 via www.methodist.org.uk/about-us/the-methodist-church/what-is-distinctive-about-methodism/a-covenant-with-god/. A. Lunn, 'Put me to doing, put me to suffering', *Theology Everywhere* (2017) accessed 23/06/2021 via https://theologyeverywhere.org/2017/02/06/put-me-to-doing-put-me-to-suffering/.

6 United Nations Department of Economic and Social Affairs (2021), 'Goal 2 | Department of Economic and Social Affairs', accessed 23/06/2021 via https://sdgs.un.org/goals/goal2.

7 Ibid.

8 F. Sosenko, M. Littlewood, G. Bramley, S. Fitzpatrick, J. Blenkinsopp, and J. Wood (2019), 'State of Hunger: A study of poverty and food insecurity in the UK' (UK: Trussel Trust), accessed 23/06/2021 via www.stateofhunger.org/wp-content/uploads/2019/11/State-of-Hunger-Report-November2019-Digital.pdf.

9 Ibid.

10 J. H. Wood (2019), 'Gender inequality: The problem of harmful, patriarchal, traditional and cultural gender practices in the church', *HTS Teologiese Studies* (Vol.75, (1), accessed 28/06/2021 via link.gale.com/apps/doc/A590915044/AONE?u=anon~5824doda&sid=googleScholar&xid=76503184.

11 R. Reddie (2011), 'British History in depth: The Church: Enslaver or Liberator?' BBC, accessed 29/06/2021 via http://www.bbc.co.uk/history/british/abolition/church_and_slavery_article_01.shtml#seven.

12 C. Pepinster (2021), 'Church excludes people with disabilities', *The Tablet* (2021), accessed 29/06/2021 via www.thetablet.co.uk/news/14128/church-excludes-people-with-disabilities-.

13 WFP (2017), 'Programme design' accessed 20/08/2021 via www.wfp.org/programme-design.

14 WFP (2017), 'World Food Assistance 2017' (Rome: UN World Food Programme).

15 WFP (2018), 'World Food Assistance 2018' (Rome: World Food Programme).

16 The Trussel Trust (2020), 'Lockdown, lifelines and the long haul ahead: The impact of Covid-19 on food banks in the Trussell Trust network', accessed 28/08/2021 via www.trusselltrust.org/wp-content/uploads/sites/2/2020/09/the-impact-of-covid-19-on-food-banks-report.pdf.

17 Ibid

18 The Food Foundation (2021), 'A Crisis Within A Crisis: The Impact of Covid-19 on Household Food Security Insights from Food Foundation Surveys on how the Pandemic has Affected Food Access in the UK', accessed 27/08/2021 via https://foodfoundation.org.uk/publication/a-crisis-within-a-crisis-the-impact-of-covid-19-on-household-food-security/.

19 The Trussel Trust, 'Lockdown, lifelines and the long haul ahead.'

20 The Food Foundation, 'A Crisis Within A Crisis.'

21 Ibid.

22 M. Young (2019), 'Busting six common myths about unconditional cash transfers in Africa', *International Food Poverty Research Institute*, accessed 25/08/2021 via www.ifpri.org/blog/busting-six-common-myths-about-unconditional-cash-transfers-africa.

23 R. Hemsteede (2018), 'Conditional or unconditional cash transfers? From ideology to policy dialogue', *Social Protection* (2018), accessed 25/08/2021 via https://socialprotection.org/discover/blog/conditional-or-unconditional-cash-transfers-ideology-policy-dialogue.

24 A. Peterman, and S. Daidone (2017), 'Evidence over Ideology: Giving Unconditional Cash in Africa – Evidence for Action', *Evidence for Action* (2017), accessed 25/08/2021 via https://blogs.unicef.org/evidence-for-action/evidence-over-ideology-giving-unconditional-cash-in-africa/; H. Wang, Q. Fang Qui, and J. Luo (2018), 'Impact of unconditional cash transfers: a replication study of the short-term effects in Kenya', *3ie Replication Paper 20* (Washington, DC: International Initiative for Impact Evaluation (3ie)). Available at: https://doi.org/10.23846/RPS0020; J. Haushofer, and J. Shapiro (2016), 'The Short-Term Impact of Unconditional Cash Transfers to the Poor: Experimental Evidence from Kenya', *The Quarterly Journal of Economics* (131 (4), 2016), pp. 1973–2042.

25 H. Westwater (2021), 'Free school meals: Everything you need to know', *The Big Issue* (2021), accessed 25/08/2021 via www.bigissue.com/latest/free-school-meals-everything-you-need-to-know/.

26 Ibid.

27 Ibid.

10

The Relevance of Mental Health for the Faith of Young People

ANNIKA MATHEWS

Human beings are complex creatures, with much to keep in equilibrium in order to be well, including our physical, emotional, mental and spiritual health. Increasingly, the pressures of our society have contributed to causing a mental health crisis across the UK. Feeling whole and happy in who we are and in what we do each day is crucial for enjoying life and feeling valued by others. The stigma that is still attached to mental health complicates the accessibility of support for those suffering. This chapter will outline why mental health is such a pertinent issue for younger generations, how the Church currently understands mental health, and how, collectively, we can begin to journey towards effective methods of helping and understanding the inclusive and complex web of mental well-being.

Mental health for young people

Younger people are particularly passionate about reaching out to those struggling with their mental health. Well-being and happiness are important at an age where a lot is in flux and people are still forging their identity and path in life. Sadly, many experience mental illness at some point in their teenage or young adult years. Increasingly, children are also presenting with symptoms of depression, anxiety or eating disorders. The Church has an opportunity to reach out to offer pastoral care and support to these young people, and I argue that it cannot effectively evangelize to them without ministering to their well-being.

I was fortunate, growing up, not to struggle with my mental health too much and was unaffected by the teenage years of angst that several of my peers experienced. However, the later years of school were harder because I (like many teenagers) struggled with the stress and pressures of exams. It was during my early years as a young adult, living independently for the first time, that I began to experience worsening mental health. Life hasn't always been easy and, despite the strengths I have from it, my dyspraxia has contributed to me over-processing things, having heightened emotions, stress and difficulties with sleep. However, I have discovered ways to manage and cope at those more difficult times and found people I trust to talk to. I explain in more detail in the next section how coming to know Christ and having a faith has helped me in my life.

Mental health: how faith can help

Personally, my faith as a Christian is a bedrock. I came to faith just before I left university, during a time where I was very fearful about the future and what lay ahead beyond the safety of education. Within the dark confusion and emptiness of my low mood and fear of the unknown, I grew restless and was searching for what came after university. I also felt something was missing in my life. Busy with various ventures alongside my degree, I was exhausted but unable to sleep that well. One of the things that attracted me was the Christian Union mission week called 'What are you searching for?' I was indeed searching for something or, as it turned out, someone: Jesus. Going along to the talks had a positive impact on me, particularly the invitation offered in John 10.10: 'I have come that they may have life, and have it to the full',[1] and I recalled a dream I'd had a month previously where I'd woken up and exclaimed: 'I believe in Jesus.' A few days after the intensity of the mission week, I had the courage and trust to say: 'Yes' to God's invitation and accepted Jesus as my saviour, faithful companion and guide onwards in the journey of life. Though I had been on a journey of exploring faith previously, I'd never felt able to believe nor perhaps realized my need for Christ as I did at that moment, shortly before many changes would take place in my life as one stage of life was to end and another begin. Those first weeks of being a Christian, I felt transformed by the peace and joy of knowing Christ, though sleep was still hard to come by. My mood was lifted, noticeably to those around me and, for a time, fears of the future subsided. However, those more difficult feelings – tearfulness, numbness, isolation and hopelessness – returned a few months later and among the changes over the last few years have continued to return.

As I have walked on the journey of faith, I have encountered mixed experiences around mental health and the Church. Although in recent years more action has been taken across society to speak about mental health, and there has been an increase in Mental Health First Aid training in workplaces, the promotion of Time to Talk days and Mental Health Awareness week, stigma still exists and awareness is mostly around more common and socially acceptable mental illnesses such as depression and anxiety.[2] In churches, a few conversations may occur and websites contain links to resources about well-being,[3] but on the whole (at least for me) it seems physical health is talked about more. Christian organizations such as ThinkTwice and the Mind and Soul Foundation run days and seminars on mental illness and well-being specifically targeted at churches, and Kintsugi Hope has begun a number of well-being support groups, including several in schools and colleges for young people, alongside those run by churches.[4] Mental illness has been made more prominent in the Church by Archbishop Justin Welby sharing his personal experiences of depression, together with other well-known people across society such as some of the Royal Family who have shown their support for talking candidly about mental health (for example, the Duke and Duchess of Cambridge have set up the initiative Heads Together).[5] However, evidenced by the backlash that Archbishop Welby received for taking a sabbatical to protect his mental health, resting is sometimes seen not as a necessity but as a luxury for clergy.[6]

What is most often appreciated by those who experience mental illness is having someone there to listen to them; someone who cares enough to be there when needed without judgement. Lighthouse West Yorkshire, connected to a church community, and the Pilsdon community, a project of communal living in a smallholding, are two examples of Christian spaces offering a welcome and home to those facing mental illness, addictions, or who are in crisis. Loneliness can often lead to a decrease in people's well-being and mental health. Loneliness is not just common in the older age groups but increasingly common among young adults, who are often dealing with quite transient lifestyles. For instance, many rent rooms in house shares, change jobs frequently in the beginning of their career (usually because of apprenticeships and short-term contracts), and travel from university to home, resulting in their living circumstances being in constant flux, which impacts on the ability to build and maintain an active social life and put down roots within a community.[7] We are created by God for companionship. Genesis 2.18 records God saying, 'It is not good for the man to be alone.' Isolation for too long, while amenable for a few, is rarely a good thing. The Covid-19 pandemic and resulting lockdowns, with the separation of families and friends, have only exacerbated the epidemic of loneliness. Although technology goes some way towards keeping people connected, it is not the same as face-to-face contact and some do not have access to the internet. Some groups have flourished during lockdown – Project Hope was set up by a few young adults and seeks to connect those aged 16–24 online with each other for conversation, a wide range of activities and social events. Telephone befriending has been a way to link people within the community as well as across the country. I phoned someone regularly for a year, after being paired up by a befriending charity.

While some parish clergy and youth workers may have limited connections with schools and universities, the importance of the school, college and university chaplaincy cannot be underestimated. Chaplains can be either ordained or lay, and seek to support teams, both spiritually and practically, across a variety of community contexts, such as educational institutions, hospitals, prisons and transport hubs. I greatly enjoyed the time I spent volunteering alongside chaplains in schools while interning at the charity Christian Youth Ministries Ipswich. Alongside providing one-to-one pastoral support and mentoring for students, the chaplains are also a source of support for staff and take a lead in offering spaces for prayer and reflection in their educational communities.[8] Though chaplaincy is on the rise, there are still too few chaplains in place and many posts are voluntary or badly paid. The Church needs to increasingly encourage chaplains in their vital ministry within the community and open further funds to support them. This mission focus is paramount considering the continuing decline in church attendance and the need to create opportunities to talk about and explore the Christian faith in a society where it is no longer the default position.

Going deeper: things the Church can improve

In its best form, the Church is a place for healing and wholeness, acceptance and inclusion. Unfortunately however, in some cases it can perpetuate the opposite. Those most vulnerable are let down and further hurt. This includes those who identify as LGBTQI+, who are often negatively impacted by their exclusion from many churches with more conservative theology. Additionally, minority groups often feel like outsiders in a congregation.[9] The Church needs to be better at embracing people where they are and celebrating them. Those with mental illnesses should feel loved and included and treated equally like fellow children of God. Like those who have physical illnesses or disabilities, it may be difficult for some experiencing mental illness to attend services in the church building. This does not mean that they should be forgotten. Instead, people should be proactive at reaching out to them and perhaps try to engage them in different ways so that they continue to feel connected to the church.

Although the Church, and those who serve it, are there for the pastoral needs of their community and congregations, among whom several individuals may be experiencing mental illness or poor mental health at any one time, in actuality mental health is not talked about in church as much as might be expected, due to the stigma surrounding it or for fear of people offending others. Some braver church leaders may address mental illness in their sermons and share their personal struggles. However, from my experience this is not done enough, despite Scripture offering a large number of examples of those who struggled with poor mental health or were experiencing extreme emotional turmoil. The beginning verses of 1 Kings 19 describe how Elijah, fearing for his life at the hands of Queen Jezebel, sat down under a broom tree in the desert and prayed to God to take his life. The book of Job describes how Job was greatly tested by events in his life. Despite remaining faithful to the Lord, he often cries out and is not at peace: for example. Job 3.26, 'I have no peace, no quietness; I have no rest, but only turmoil.' The writers of the Psalms poured out their mental anguish, desperation and emotional pain to God amid the difficult circumstances they found themselves in: Psalm 88.3, 'I am overwhelmed with troubles and my life draws near to death' and Psalm 88.18, 'darkness is my closest friend'. Though the context of these writings differed, the emotions and thoughts expressed in the psalms are timeless. Jesus experienced unimaginable mental and emotional suffering, most notably in the Garden of Gethsemane where he says to those disciples who are with him, 'My soul is deeply grieved, to the point of death' (Matt. 26.38), and later, as he was dying on the cross, loudly crying out '"Eloi, Eloi, lema sabachthani"

– which means, "My God, my God, why have you forsaken me?"' (Matt. 27.46).

If mental illness and mental health are not talked about openly on a regular basis, they become a taboo subject which has to be hidden and only reserved for individual, private pastoral conversations. The reality is that many people struggle with their mental health, to varying extents. Anyone can experience mental illness and everyone has mental health. Though depression and anxiety tend to be talked about more, other mental illnesses, such as bipolar disorder, eating disorders, psychosis, schizophrenia and personality disorders, are avoided. There needs to be more space created for conversations about mental health and well-being, as well as stories shared by those with lived experience of different mental illnesses and an acknowledgement that no two people's experiences of having a mental illness are the same.

We find that one of our biggest discussion taboos, somewhat unusually for a faith where death is otherwise often considered, is the discussion around suicide and the experience of suicidal thoughts, the latter more common than realized. Of course, this needs to be done in a sensitive manner, yet avoiding it and treating it as the elephant in the room only contributes to a culture of silence, where those who need support may not feel able to reach out for fear of what people may say. On a training day for a Youth Mental Health First Aid course, I was shocked how few people put their hand up when asked if they would be comfortable bringing up the topic of suicide or knowing how to respond if someone told them they were thinking of ending their life.[10] While people who die by suicide are lamented, those experiencing suicidal thoughts are not always given the care they need. This is in spite of the fact that according to statistics from a survey conducted across homes in England in 2014, within a person's lifetime at least 1 in 5 people have suicidal thoughts, 1 in 14 people self-harm and 1 in 15 people attempt suicide.[11] Unfortunately, rates among young people are on the increase. Recently, there has been a focus on the news of student suicide at universities and the negative impact of the pandemic restrictions on students' mental health.[12] The 2019 Office for National Statistics data showed that in nine years 174 students in England and Wales had taken their lives.[13]

Being within the institutional structures of the Church of England through the discernment process has been rather eye-opening. Although conversations about well-being and mental health are filtering into church congregations at grass-roots levels, behind the scenes mental illness is still often painted in a negative light. Overall, I feel more needs to be done by the Church to take care of its own ministers. Too often clergy give out pastoral care to those they minister to, experiencing huge drains on their time and emotional reserves, yet they are expected to look after their own mental health by means of their individual support networks. Although there are some diocesan counselling services and mental health support services available for clergy to access, the Church as employer needs to put more funding into these services to support the well-being of its officeholders and employees. Too many suffer in silence, perhaps because they are expected to be strong and fear what will happen if they are seen to not be coping. The life of the minister is a demanding one but there is no reason why someone with a mental illness should not be able to fulfil the role as well as anyone else. Having a mental illness does not render one incapable of ministering effectively. It should not be seen as a sign of weakness or fragility to require support from mental health services, be that a form of therapy or medication. Rather, the recognition that help is required should be seen as a positive sign of self-awareness.

The concept of 'The Wounded Healer' has been used to talk about Christ and his ministry; he bore not only the physical scars from his whipping and crucifixion but also mental and emotional scars. He can empathize with our pain. So too, 'we all to some extent are wounded' but can learn 'how to put our woundedness to the service of others', and gradually heal as we serve.[14] Often those who have experienced mental illness or poor mental health will be more understanding and accepting of others' struggles, and be ready to listen and support them as far as possible. Ministers are no exception to that, and carrying someone else's burdens is very different to dealing with one's own.

Although medication and secular psychotherapy are mostly viewed well, there are still some in the Church who view them with suspicion or view mental illness as a sign of weak faith or character. Recommended activities for improving well-being, the focus on the Northern European state of hygge and self-help books, which have all become increasingly popular in recent years, are seen by some in the Church as contrary to or separate from Christian faith practices. The practice of mindfulness,[15] as well as other forms of exercise and relaxation such as meditation and yoga, have been viewed with suspicion or seen as incompatible with the Christian faith because several of these practices originate from Buddhism, although they have since been capitalized on by well-being practitioners who have secularized them and removed them from the authenticity of the complex and illuminating context of Eastern philosophy and religion. Nevertheless, for me mindfulness played a part in opening my mind to what might be going on in my life and around me, creating space for quiet reflection in an otherwise busy world. I do not think it was coincidence that I became a Christian at the time I was doing mindfulness – I like to think I was trying to become more self-aware and perceptive of my thoughts and God used it as part of what opened my mind to discovering Jesus. Some of the grounding and meditative techniques are complementary to Ignatian-style meditation and forms of creative prayer and exercises from the contemplative traditions (in Jesuit spirituality, for example), which helps us become more aware of God's presence in the world around us.[16] The Examen and stilling prayers share many similarities to mindfulness.

Looking after ourselves is not idolatry or neglect of God but an awareness of how precious we are in God's eyes and an appreciation of the gift of life. Denying ourselves does not equate with neglecting ourselves. The promotion of resting, getting sufficient sleep or maintaining some sort of Sabbath is biblically attested (see the creation story, Gen. 2.2–3). Being busy has become endemic in society and sometimes doing is valued more than being. This mindset infiltrates faith and church too, where positions on church rotas need to be filled, and it can seem that those doing roles are sometimes valued more than those who participate in church life by being in the congregation. Though doing and serving can help people thrive and use their gifts, the creation of space in the day to just be, pause and reflect (the practice of selah) is important for our well-being and affects how we can effectively fulfil our God-given roles and grow in faith as we spend time with God and one another. The story of Martha and Mary, with their respective roles of doing and being (Luke 10.38–42), reflects the importance of this. Jesus visits the two sisters at home and they react very differently. While Martha busies herself preparing the house for their guest, Mary sits at Jesus' feet, listening to his words. Martha appears perturbed by the fact Mary is not helping her with her work but Jesus tells Martha she is concerned with too many things and Mary is focused on the one thing which matters most: her relationship with God. Jesus often goes off by himself to pray, away from the disciples and the crowd before and after his ministry (see Luke 5.16 and Matt. 14.22–23). Time spent alone with God the Father provides Jesus with rejuvenation, and likely, time to refocus his attention before each ministry task. Silence can seem a scary prospect to some people but equally can be liberating.

It goes without saying that there is no place for people to judge others or spout theology at them and, certainly, when they are struggling with mental illness is not the time to question the depth of a person's faith. Struggling with symptoms of a mental illness does not make someone weak; indeed, it often indicates their resilience and strength to keep going and their sensitivities to a broken world. I myself appreciate praying with those I trust when I'm at my lowest and also receiving healing prayer. However, no single form of care fits all and when praying for others, we must choose our words carefully in order to help, and not hurt, one another. It is vital that prayer is not forced upon others who may not feel comfortable and that the power dynamics within any time of prayer are considered. Notions of spiritual attack, or sin connected to a person's state of mental health are nearly always unhelpful, as they propagate a narrative of guilt and shame and can cause deeper pain and emotional damage. So, too, it is not the case that those of faith experiencing periods of poor mental health are any less of a Christian disciple or less able to hear God. There can be times (whether in poor or good mental health) where God seems more distant or I feel less connected to my faith and feel unable to live it out. At other points, God seems very close. However, throughout these times my knowledge of God is unaffected. My ability to discern God is also not necessarily affected by the state of my mental health, as I came to faith in Christ when experiencing a very low mood.

Those in the Church should consider their use of theology and Bible verses carefully when speaking to those experiencing periods of poor mental health or mental illness. Some things shared may be well-meaning yet impose seemingly unattainable limits and pressure on people at a difficult time. When someone's self-esteem is crushed and they feel unlovable and unworthy, one hopes that others will reach out and demonstrate how much they are worth to them through actions and words. A reminder of the expanse of God's unconditional love for them and the preciousness to God of their existence just as they are is often sufficient, though silence and a space for quiet reflection may also be appropriate. More often than not, what is needed at these times is for people just to be present pastorally, offering a listening, non-judgmental ear or practical support and a willingness to come alongside others, whatever they are going through.

Conclusion

Steps are being taken in the right direction towards creating a culture whereby people feel able to talk about mental health in church and society and relate it to faith. Many initiatives exist to facilitate this and hopefully more will be created in light of the heightened mental health crisis resulting from the coronavirus pandemic. However, conversations need to turn to active support, and more can always be done. In church, where one hopes that people would be able to share without judgement, fear often still reigns, and many hide their struggles from others. Until it becomes common to reply truthfully to that most dreaded of questions 'How are you?' and the maintenance of mental health and discussion about mental illness are mainstream, it is going to remain difficult for those with mental illness or who experience periods of poor mental health to feel able to be fully themselves in church, in both good and bad times. Furthermore, if we cannot authentically be our full selves in our congregations and share both our joys and sorrows with one another, we are not modelling Christ's community.[17]

Notes

1 This and the following Bible references are all from the NIV translation.

2 The Mental Health Foundation runs Mental Health Awareness Week, www.mentalhealth.org.uk/our-work and Rethink Mental Illness promote Time to Talk events www.rethink.org/

3 See, for example, the Church of England mental health resources: www.churchofengland.org/resources/mental-health-resources; and a report on how to have a conversation about mental health produced by the URC Youth Assembly, https://urc.org.uk/good-news-stories/2041-get-talking-starting-conversations-about-mental-wellbeing.html

4 Christian organizations focused on well-being include:
Mind and Soul Foundation: www.mindandsoulfoundation.org/.
Kintsugi Hope: www.kintsugihope.com/.
Think Twice: https://thinktwiceinfo.org/.

5 E. Barnett, 'Interview with Justin Welby: I felt nervous about opening up about my mental health', *BBC News*, accessed 11/06/2021 via www.bbc.co.uk/news/av/health-50576345.

6 For example, see K. Armstrong, 'Dear Archbishop, now is not the time to take a sabbatical', *The Guardian* (25/11/2020) accessed 11/06/2021 via www.theguardian.com/commentisfree/2020/nov/25/archbishop-of-canterbury-justin-welby-sabbatical-pandemic-religion.

7 J. Arnett, *Emerging Adulthood: The Winding Road from the Late Teens Through the Twenties* (2nd edn, Oxford: Oxford University Press, 2015).

8 See Chapter 12, which discusses Sophie Mitchell's experiences of working as the University of Bristol's Multifaith Chaplaincy Assistant.

9 See Chapter 3 where Nosa Idehen discusses inter-racial relations.

10 Mental Health First Aid England offers training courses tailored for youth mental health and adult mental health: https://mhfaengland.org/. The charity Papyrus offers advice and support for under-35s experiencing suicidal thoughts or affected by suicide: www.papyrus-uk.org/ (accessed 11/06/2021).

11 S. McManus, P. Bebbington, R. Jenkins and T. Brugha, 'Adult Psychiatric Morbidity Survey: Survey of Mental Health and Well-being', *NHS Digital* (30/09/2016), accessed 03/06/2021 via https://webarchive.nationalarchives.gov.uk/ukgwa/20180328140249/http:/digital.nhs.uk/catalogue/PUB21748

12 S. Coughlan, 'Would Universities Call Parents in a Mental Health Crisis?' *BBC News*, accessed 11/05/2021 via www.bbc.co.uk/news/education-56763189.

13 See 'Suicides in full-time students aged 18 years and above, by sex, registered in England and Wales between 2010 and 2019', *Office for National Statistics*, accessed 11/05/2021 via www.ons.gov.uk/peoplepopulationandcommunity/birthsdeathsandmarriages/deaths/adhocs/12336suicidesinfulltimestudentsaged18yearsandabove-bysexregisteredinenglandandwalesbetween2010and2019.

14 H. J. Nouwen, *The Wounded Healer* (New York: Doubleday Image Books, 1972).

15 For an introduction to mindfulness see www.mindful.org/meditation/mindfulness-getting-started/.

16 See the Jesuits website for Ignatian spirituality resources: www.pathwaystogod.org/resources.

17 If you have found any of the above content distressing or have concerns about your own mental health, or that of someone you know, the following websites may be helpful to you: Young Minds (for under 25s), https://youngminds.org.uk/; Mind, www.mind.org.uk/ and Samaritans, www.samaritans.org/.

'The Intentional Integration of Homeless and Formally Homeless Communities Radically Transforms the Life of Our Church'

SHERMARA J. J. FLETCHER

Introduction

On any journey, there comes a crucial point where it is wise to pause, take stock of what has been and actively reflect and plan what will come ahead. This advice does not solely apply to journeys of self-discovery but to civic, state and market-led institutions and especially to the Church. This chapter will focus on the opportunity that churches can take in renavigating and reimagining their engagement with and perceptions of the homeless communities they serve and will argue that when the Church takes seriously the capacity of homeless leaders (which I have phrased as 'unlikely leaders') their spaces become transformed. The term 'homelessness' in this chapter will refer to those without permanent accommodation, and principally rough sleepers who are often institutionalized to the streets, experience severe mental, spiritual and physical health issues and are often perceived as a social hazard.

When churches take this journey of faith to include the homeless in the life, leadership and teaching of their church, not only do their cultures become radically inclusive, but they are brought to a truer light of what the Church is, who they are, and most importantly who God is.

Let the journey begin

My journey of discovery, engagement and friendship with the homeless community began at the age of 18 when I was awakened in a Sunday morning service to the reality that the *missio dei* takes place beyond the four walls of the church. The local evangelist at the time, an 80-year-old minister called Hamilton whose youth shone through his attire and personality, shared his life-transforming ministry with the homeless, incarcerated and those on the fringes of society who constantly faced marginalization. Compelled by Hamilton's testimony I found myself serving at his food bank the following month. Honouring this conviction changed my life's trajectory and was one of the first times I had experienced God beyond the pages of the Bible and the formalities of a Sunday service.

However, on this journey I had many lessons to learn. As a younger Christian I was full of zeal and passion and enraged by the injustice that a first-world, economically advanced country had people sleeping on the streets. Some would have called me a 'woke snowflake' and I would have worn that cultural label with honour. Armed and ready to live out the call in Luke 4.18 to 'preach the gospel to the poor' and heal the broken-hearted while setting the oppressed free, my first evening with Hamilton quickly turned from a night of expectant enthusiasm and impact to a lesson in humility and a stark realization that God's activity was already present. I was astonished to walk into a strong, yet simultaneously fragile community. Those experiencing homelessness were helping each other, sharing the limited resources and food they had while not knowing where the next meal would come from. That evening there were former teachers, university lecturers, a former local politician, people who had gone through a difficult divorce or had lost a close family member, people from different ethnicities and walks of life. There were also homeless Christians who would help share the gospel and distribute the meals.

This bustling subculture embodied a generosity and selfless-ness that was often difficult to find in mainstream society. They didn't need my well-meaning 'young woke Christian zeal', where I already thought I had all the solutions and answers, but wanted community, dignity, and reciprocal interactions where their stories and knowledge were equally valued and where encounters did not objectify them for extracting food or money. It became clear that I had come to participate in God's mission, not to create it, and have been tasked since with help-ing churches to do the same. If Christians are really going to live up to challenging injustice, the concept of being woke can be a catalyst for our personal action, but it cannot end there, it is not enough. Often activism actually does more for the activ-ist than the community it is trying to help. Christians need to go beyond activism and speaking on behalf of others, towards working alongside those who are marginalized to change and transform structures, not apart from the communities that are the object of our concern but with and through them. We also need to be open and humble enough to be positively impacted and changed in the process by those we may con-sider disadvantaged. In fact, they may have many privileges and qualities that as younger Christians we can take hope from and have an opportunity to learn from. Being 'woke' as a Christian therefore should not be an individualistic identity marker. Instead, it should concern the curation of a communal identity that is fighting for a larger change.

Another important lesson on my journey and interaction with the homeless community was the move from charity to justice. This was strongly influenced through my engagement with community organizing, where I learnt that the injustices faced by homeless people were not to be solely tackled through advocacy, as this would place me at the centre of the change and I would be speaking on behalf of the homeless. This then raised the critical question, how do you provide space for their authentic voice? How do you appropriately support vulnerable people who need help without culturally colonizing their narrative, lived experience and agency to be a part of the change against the injustices they face and ultimately to be the centre of their own story?

As I continued my journey this question was reconciled through the deeper study of the principles of community organizing, which state:

1 Help people to develop their collective power to act together for the common good of the whole community.
2 Build on what already exists if that is what the community needs and wants, and co-operate with others.
3 Put the well-being, development, and progress of people first.
4 Take responsibility for maintaining the quality and ethos of community organizing.
5 Work for a just society.
6 Demonstrate honesty and integrity and uphold public trust and confidence.
7 Demonstrate respect for diversity and promote equality.
8 Do not do for others what they can do for themselves.[1]

Principle 8 of community organizing helped cultivate a 'power with', as opposed to a 'power over' or 'power for', model which was the first step in developing the leadership, agency and dignity of homeless communities which would then help them to reintegrate into society and the Church.

As my work with homeless communities developed, it became important to establish reciprocity in all encounters. By this I mean the ability to foster appropriate mutual relationships and humbly learn and appropriately receive from those experiencing homelessness as well as give. It was also important to honour and value their humanity with the understanding that they were more than their homelessness status. It also became fundamental to ensure that their dignity was honoured and that they were not paternalized. Working with homeless communities also taught me to challenge capitalist notions of human meritocracy and the value placed on economic productivity and that I should actively work to close the 'housed and homeless' divide of them and us.

Theopraxis of the homeless

The Church can learn more about its mission and God by learning from the theopraxis of homeless and formerly homeless Christians as well as the spirituality of poorer communities. In this chapter, theopraxis is defined as the observation of God in the context of his actions, and how it impacts people's real life in the here and now. Many homeless and formerly homeless Christians who have not been educationally trained often subscribe to this theological understanding of God in which they operate outside of academic ways of knowing. Alternative expressions such as the arts, intuition, a disciplined prayer life, a high view of Scripture and the prophetic often form ways of articulating God. Furthermore, homeless Christians and non-Christian homeless communities often rely on God for their very basic human needs. His action is expected and needed in their physical material and immediate need.

I witnessed the theopraxis of homeless and formerly homeless people in my work in East London, where the Church created non-cerebral Bible studies through painting, pictures and music. This not only enabled different ways of knowing but democratized the theological understanding of God. It also opened the group and wider Church to new revelations of God's activity in the world as well as in their personal lives. The democratization also built their confidence and even created space for different vocations of homeless, formerly homeless and vulnerable individuals to be birthed and taken seriously. This resulted in an unlikely leader we were working with one Sunday afternoon expressing, 'I feel called to the homeless', and training was put in place for him to live out God's call in his life.

A radical inclusivity

The Gospel of John's account of Jesus declaring his mission and ministry, and the use of food to metaphorically convey the incarnational nature of his relationship with humanity, helps us to examine Jesus' idea of inclusivity as well as his radical hospitality. John 6.35–36 shares, 'Whoever comes to me will never go hungry, and whoever believes in me will never be thirsty.' The use of the pronoun 'whoever', '*nas*' in Greek, implies everyone, all, and emphasizes the level of inclusivity at Jesus' table, including homeless people, and especially rough sleepers who often suffer from extreme mental, physical and spiritual health difficulties.

The Lord's communion goes beyond the symbolic ritual of Jesus' last supper. German theologian Helmut Goliwitzer explored the link between the communion and the homeless/marginalized through his observations that

> those who have eaten of the body of the Lord are looked on as one man and so if there is a hungry Christian who is experiencing hardship and homelessness wherever they are in the world, then this is a misery that the whole Christian fellowship should feel as the communion makes us one.[2]

His insight implies a radical mutual accountability between Christians. The Church should practise Christian *diakonia*, which is a deeper type of *koinonia* that describes a community that 'works for the welfare of all its members as well as helping to build the reign of God throughout the entire world'.[3] This implies that homeless and hungry people should be wholly inside the structures of established churches.

The Church is gifted in providing food banks and support to homeless people in the UK. Churches should be commended for the social capital they contribute to providing spaces for the welfare of the homeless, but are most of these spaces alternative ones that operate outside the main congregational gathering on a Sunday? And if so, why? Are churches willing to disrupt their programmes and for their spaces to be transformed in a non-romanticized way by the full presence, participation and even leadership of homeless communities/individuals of faith? Inderjit Boghol engages with this debate about inclusivity, and reflecting Matthew 15.21–28, she paints

> [m]y vision of church and community pictures God's table and banquet, which has room for all people, of all nations, of all ages. God's respect and God's embrace desires life for everyone. Human selfishness creates destructive strategies, which give pride of place to a chosen few at the Table and place the rest underneath it to eat the scraps that fall off or are thrown at them. In Jesus, God shows us the way to end these strategies so that all may sit and eat together at the Table for all.[4]

It can be argued that the Church generally struggles to integrate the homeless into its wider life, leadership, teaching structures and theological production due to the temptation to inhabit solely a paternalistic role and perception that the homeless are solely dependants. This attitude can create a non-reciprocal environment and quench the reality and revelation that homeless communities can bring to the journey of faith. Understandably, churches and church leaders may genuinely be taking into consideration the vulnerability involved in a homeless individual's life and may be wary of placing responsibilities during this unsettling time. However, Helmut Goliwitzer shares a different interpretation of why churches may struggle with genuine engagement and integration, through his insight that 'the baptized persons sit as rich men in well covered tables, and poor unbaptized Lazarus lies outside at the door – really outside, and therefore even more powerless, easier to be passed over at our meal'.[5] Goliwitzer exposes that there is a lack of value put on those without material wealth and feeds the narrative that the homeless disrupt the trendy branding and culture of churches that will detract audiences that churches 'truly' want and that can financially contribute.

Angus Ritchie delves deeper into this exploration through his insight that, '[i]t's not enough to be a church with "a heart for the poor"',[6] which suggests that the church should not solely have sentiment and operate based on an unhealthy dynamic of paternalism but calls for a more radical commitment of genuine relationship, linking to the necessity of reciprocity in value as explained throughout this chapter. It also supports the position that the homeless should also be at the centre, help make decisions, that space is made for their voice to impact the lives of other Christians and ultimately to be key contributors in the church's life and revival.

Theologian, Ruben Arjona-Mejia, also engages in this debate by challenging the value-based dichotomy between 'the haves/housed' and 'have nots/homeless' and the perception that the homeless cannot contribute to the wider life and leadership of the church beyond the foodbank. He reminds us that 'The patriarchs, like men of our time, are not just patriarchal; they are also homeless exiles and pilgrims possessed of profound faith and hope. Who is yanked into more unsettled and tormented lives than figures like Adam, Noah, Abraham, Isaac, Esau, Jacob, Joseph, Moses, Jesus, Paul?'[7]

The leadership development of homeless communities for the revitalization of our Church

Taking the theopraxis and the radical inclusivity of homeless and former homeless people seriously, integrating their understanding and knowing of God into the life and teaching of our churches helps the Church to uncover the value of leaders like Jesus' first disciple Peter, and not to idolize cerebral leaders like Paul. Both styles are of value and bring vitality to the Church and an imbalance mars the full image of God's Ecclesia. One of the pathways to doing this is by creating a missional focus on the leadership development of homeless and formerly homeless people through what I call the 'unlikely leader'. By unlikely leader I mean those who may be overlooked or underestimated in society because they do not fit mainstream or traditional perceptions of leadership and may have experienced a form of vulnerability in their life. When this brave and bold move is taken and the Church enjoys the fruits of unlikely leaders in our communities, it changes our Church because the full image of God is expressed and expands. The Church of England's Archbishop's Council speaks into the importance of this and states,

> Until laity and clergy/church leaders are convinced, based on their baptismal mutuality, that they are equal in worth and status, complementary in gifting and vocation, mutually accountable in discipleship, and equal partners in mission, we will never form Christian communities that can evangelize the nation.[8]

When one-dimensional perceptions of Christian leadership are dismantled and the vocational value of homeless Christians is taken seriously, not only will this transform how we do mission, but it will also sustain the mission by expanding the gifts involved and cultivating a healthy rhythm and expectation that mission is not the responsibility of a few.

East London

As my journey continued, my time of grassroot engagement with homeless communities in East London presented additional lessons to my night with Hamilton. I was amazed at the impact produced in our mission when we intentionally developed those who would usually be overlooked. Out of my typologies of unlikely leaders, this rest of this chapter will focus on 'The Often-Powerless Unlikely Leader'.

Unlikely leaders, who often experience powerlessness through multiple circumstances in their daily lives, are not only a gift to the church and its mission but can be spiritual and cultural transformers of church institutions. This includes individuals who have overcome trauma and addiction, former homeless and currently homeless individuals, those who experience poor working conditions and wages and often have less agency in their everyday life. Often these unlikely leaders are seen as those whom the church helps, and this is appropriate at times, but it is not the sole purpose of our interaction. Intentionally building relationship with this type of leader is transformational because many powerless, unlikely leaders are used to interactions where they are solely the beneficiary, are felt sorry for and their identity if often linked to their vulnerability.

Luke 5.11 highlights the importance of developing unlikely leaders in and for our mission in the account of Jesus choosing his first disciple, Peter. It is interesting that Jesus' first choice for his top team cabinet is a fisherman. Visiting the temple regularly for the annual festivals he would have seen the rabbis and leaders of the temple and could have sought to align himself with a political leader of power who would compound his influence, or even with the socialites of his day, yet he chooses a simple fisherman. I cannot imagine that he would have looked or smelled the part.

This text highlights a few key themes, especially for those who are leading the development of homeless ministries and want to integrate the homeless into the life of the church:

1 Unlikely leaders often do not esteem themselves or are quick to disqualify themselves due to their perceived lack of stature. When Peter is approached, he points out his flaws very quickly: 'Simon answered, "Master, we've worked hard all night and haven't caught anything" ... When Simon Peter saw this, he fell at Jesus' knees and said, "Go away from me, Lord; I am a sinful man!"' Yet Jesus sees great potential and publicly affirms Peter. Peter goes on to build and establish the Church, and our mission is a fruit of his fishing.

2 When finding an unlikely leader, dare yourself to see beyond their current position, role, or perspective and help them to see that they are needed for the mission.

3 Developing the unlikely leader pushes the church to genuinely look at what it takes for their development, even
if it means repositioning the church's programme. It is as
much about the process as about the result. The value of
the powerless, unlikely leader is evident when institutional
systems are in place to take seriously their development,
growth and vocation. They may also operate in a different way of knowing and understanding and may process
information differently.

And the questions for us today are: Are we willing to change
our structures and cultures of learning so that everyone can
participate in the mission? And are we willing to create access
for their vocation to flourish in our church and missional programmes as well as being open to them helping to shape and
influence our culture?

When working in East London, we developed The Open
Table at St George in the East Church, which still runs today
and 'is comprised of a leadership team of former homeless,
homeless and housed individuals. This has helped to develop
unlikely leaders, who experience powerlessness in everyday
life, and has enabled them to find their vocation. It has also
helped the church to reach new disciples and transformed the
church to see more of the Kingdom of God. However, this kind
of project involves:

1 Patience.
2 Being okay with things being a bit messy, or not the status
quo, and the curation of a space that allows room for
mistakes.
3 Open humility to see God manifest in a different way.
4 Leadership who are open to getting involved, and making
space for, and learning from, unlikely leaders.
5 Resisting the assumption that the Holy Spirit is not already
working and speaking in more fragile and vulnerable communities.

6 Not being hard on yourself and making additional space to speak to a spiritual director to vent and discuss any impact this has on yourself.

So, as I reflect on the journey so far, I finish this chapter by encouraging you, at whatever stage of the journey you are on, to reflect deeply on how you and your church engage with individuals experiencing homelessness, particularly those who are street homeless. I also encourage you to find the hope and justice that comes when churches and individuals resist the temptation of operating in woke individualism – by placing oneself at the centre of change – and woke paternalism – by treating homeless communities solely as beneficiaries to be cared for. If instead we see and treat homeless individuals as co-creators in the churches' vision and mission, our churches may become woke spaces of collective transformation.

When churches are willing to venture into this risky enterprise of taking the spirituality and theopraxis of the homeless community seriously, it erodes and resists monolithic representation of the Christian experience by those who teach the church. It illuminates a fuller picture of God, his heart and desire to give agency to the poor and those who are homeless. It is a journey worth taking.

Notes

1 Community Organisers, 'Our Principles', accessed 26/08/2021 via www.corganisers.org.uk/what-is-community-organising/co-principles-of-practice/.

2 H. Gollwitzer, trans. D. Cairns, *The Rich Christians and Poor Lazarus* (Edinburgh: St Andrew Press, 1974), p. 5.

3 J. Kelly, 'Catholic Virtual Schools: Real Possibilities or Oxymoronic Dreams?' *Journal of Catholic Education* (Vol. 5 (4), 2020), p. 427.

4 I. S. Bhogal, *A Table for All: A Challenge to Church and Nation* (Sheffield: Penistone Publications, 2000), p. 12.

5 Goliwitzer, *The Rich Christians*, p. 8.

6 A. Ritchie, 'People of Power: How community organising recalls the Church to the Vision of The Gospel' (London: The Centre of Theology and Community, 2018) pp. 1–38, p. 7, accessed 26/03/2021 via http://www.theology-centre.org.uk/wp-content/uploads/2013/04/People-of-Power-.pdf.

7 R. Arjona-Mejia, 'Hoagies and Tacos: Food and Men's Unquenchable Hunger', *Pastoral Psychology* (Vol. 64 (3), 2014), pp. 297–310, p. 305.

8 A Report from the Archbishops' Council, 'Setting God's People Free' (n.d) accessed 26/08/2021 via www.churchofengland.org/sites/default/files/2017-11/gs-2056-setting-gods-people-free.pdf.

12

Interfaith Engagement as Social Action: Going Beyond Sharing Samosas to Realizing a Common Humanity

SOPHIE MITCHELL

Every year, the Multifaith Chaplaincy at the University of Bristol hosts the Faith Crawl, giving staff and students an opportunity to learn about different faith and spiritual communities by taking them on a tour of local faith centres. At the University of Bristol it is easy to live in the bubble of Clifton and Redland, rarely venturing outside a five-mile radius of the campus. The Faith Crawl allows staff and students to discover a different Bristol, one that is overflowing with diverse traditions of faith and spirituality. Past Faith Crawls have included visits to a Baha'i centre and a progressive synagogue, and a talk from a local humanist representative.

It is not just the opportunity to learn about different faith and spiritual communities that makes the Faith Crawl so special. It is the conversations with other attendees, either en route between the different stops or over a delicious vegetarian curry shared at the end. Not everyone on the Faith Crawl identifies with a particular faith or spirituality, but there is a common fascination with, and willingness to learn about, different beliefs and practices. It was events like the Faith Crawl that led me to carry on my interfaith work through the position of Chaplaincy Assistant at the University of Bristol Multifaith Chaplaincy, after completing my undergraduate degree.

At the heart of this chapter is the point that *all interfaith engagement can be defined as social action, in that it brings different people together to build a better world.* By 'better' I mean a world that is connected, accepting and generous – one in which people from different backgrounds live and flourish alongside each other and everyone is uniquely valued. I truly believe that in spending time with people of other faiths and spiritualities, we are each doing our part in local, national and global efforts to improve the world.

Before we start, we must clarify what counts as interfaith engagement. Some argue that the interaction must involve intentional or expert reflection of theology.[1] However, this approach creates barriers to engagement, making it harder for non-experts to get involved. Intentional theological reflection does have importance but should not be misconceived as the only type of engagement. Interfaith engagement is part of everyday life, occurring every time people of different faiths meet and interact. It is an unavoidable reality, in that we are all involved in interfaith every day in our schools, universities and workplaces, as the Board for Mission and Unity of the Church of England summarized, 'dialogue as a way of life, a personal encounter in the community. Where families meet as neighbours, where children play together and where men and women work side-by-side or stand together in the unemployment queue, dialogue is related to the whole of life.'[2]

Contextualizing interfaith

Though people of different faiths and spiritualities have been living and working together throughout history, interfaith was not formally recognized until the meeting of the Parliament of World's Religions in 1893, which brought together religious leaders from around the world. This was followed by the World Missionary Conference of Edinburgh 1910, which, through Commission IV, affirmed that Christians should approach people from other religions with sensitivity and should take time to learn about their histories and traditions.[3] This initial model of interfaith emphasized dialogue between, and theological comparison of, different religions. However, it was not long before a gradual shift occurred in the way we do interfaith, from talking *about* different religions to talking *with* different religions.[4] A significant factor in this shift can be attributed to global efforts by young people in student Christian movements to engage with social justice issues that affected people of other religions and spiritualities.[5] This new approach to interfaith engagement was solidified and became normal practice after the second Vatican Council, especially with the declaration of *Nostra Aetate*,[6] and has fundamentally changed the way that different religions view and interact with each other, reflecting a shift from competitors to potential partners.[7] In the UK, this method is exemplified in the establishment of the Council of Christians and Jews in 1942, the Inter Faith Network for the UK in 1987, and hundreds of local or regional interfaith councils. Today, interfaith engagement is required for two reasons: our increasing multi-faith reality and rising religious intolerance.

Towards the end of the twentieth century, the secularization thesis was prominent, hypothesizing that the more we modernize as a society, the less religious we become.[8] Though there has been a decrease in Christianity in the traditional denominations and an increase in atheism, the 36th British Social Attitudes survey also shows that there has been an increase in non-Christian religions.[9] Our increasing multi-faith reality creates many opportunities to improve our world. However, it is also unfortunately paired with rising religious intolerance. You only need to speak to friends, neighbours or colleagues from minority religious communities to understand the scale and reality of Islamophobia, anti-Semitism and other forms of religious discrimination. This is partially due to the false representations of religious life in the media, which reinforce false stereotypes and generate fear. These representations fail to take into account the 'untold stories' of countless individuals who, motivated by faith, are working to make the world a better place.[10] The reality of our increasing multi-faith world, paired with rising religious intolerance, has created an urgent need for interfaith engagement. We must all reflect on what it means to live in this multi-faith reality, whether we are people of faith or not. Fortunately, as well as being the reason why we need to engage in interfaith, our multi-faith reality is also the means to do so, by creating opportunities to learn about different faith and spiritualities from the local communities themselves; it is its own solution.[11]

Interfaith dialogue as social action

There are different ways of doing interfaith engagement, typically fitting into three main categories: educative, social and immersive. Some interfaith engagement covers all these categories. The Faith Crawl is a perfect example of this, where attendees learn about the different faiths and spiritualities (educative) by visiting centres (immersive), and then reflect on their experiences over a hearty vegetarian curry (social). How and where does social action fit into this?

The UK government defines social action as people coming together to make a positive difference in their communities by working to solve local issues.[12] People of different faiths and spiritualities often come together to run interfaith social action projects, to raise money for charity, volunteer and stand against discrimination. While these do, of course, make a positive contribution to a local community, long-term social change is created by the relationships built through the planning and running of these projects, as well as other types of interfaith events. Pratt explains:

> [M]uch of positive value is achieved when people of different faiths work together for the common good. Much more can yet happen when people of different faiths sit down together

to share, in depth, the riches of their spiritual resources, and when they learn both to listen to and respectfully critique one another.[13]

In 2019, I was part of a committee of students from different faith societies who came together to organize and run a hugely successful programme of events for Interfaith Week. From panel discussions, to an interfaith meditation session, to the Big Interfaith Quiz of the Year, the week was a celebration of the religious diversity on campus. Though our aim was to bring students of different faith backgrounds together, it was actually working closely with the other faith reps to deliver the events that I most valued. Rather than the particular project being understood as social action, it is the counter-cultural act of being with others who are different to yourself that is social action. In defining interfaith engagement as social action, I posit that there are two short-term methods, promoting better understanding and celebrating diversity, which lead to two long-term outcomes. building bridges and relationships and realizing a common humanity. The next section will unpack these methods and outcomes.

Promoting better understanding

Many societal problems stem from a lack of understanding and fear of the unknown. In his Introduction to Gaston's book, E. Graham summarizes Gaston's theory that the process of secularization, and I would add radical secularism, has caused us to become religiously illiterate and unable to deal with our increasingly multi-faith world.[14] Even younger people who have grown up in a more diverse society than previous generations often base their understanding of different faiths and spiritualities on over-simplistic judgements and sweeping generalizations taught in schools, such as 'all Catholics support abortion' and 'all Muslim women wear the Hijab or Burka'.

The first step is to tackle these misconceptions, and the

prejudice generated from them, by promoting better understanding and a fair and nuanced representation of diverse faiths and spiritualities. This can be attempted either through dedicated events that explain what different faiths or spiritualities teach, or through simply spending time with people who are different to ourselves. Encountering difference allows us to appreciate why people believe what they believe and live as they do, and forces us to discover that we may have held false representations of different religions.[15] When we come together, talk to and listen to those from other backgrounds, we realize what is true and false about their beliefs, practices and motives. Then, 'as our understanding grows so we are able to counter prejudice and both innocent and malicious rumours. We come to a clear understanding of our similarities and differences.'[16] In my experience of Chaplaincy, it has been essential to create safe spaces, formal and informal, for these similarities and differences to be explored between students. In this space, there is always room for mistake, growth and learning. Here, Sudworth comments, 'when we get it wrong, as we will, it will become an occasion for laughter and intimacy rather than of suspicion and an enmity'.[17] In creating and facilitating this space, the Chaplaincy helps students better respect and value diverse faiths and spiritualities, and do this exploration confidently.[18]

Celebrating diversity

In promoting a better understanding, interfaith engagement encourages us to think about where there is overlap and where there is profound difference. As humans, we tend to see difference as a threat. However, interfaith celebrates diversity as something that allows individuals and communities to flourish. When we let down our defence barriers, we allow ourselves to learn about the beauty and uniqueness of different traditions, arriving at a place of honouring difference rather than merely tolerating it. Disagreements may occur, but they are embraced respectfully, rather than attempted to be resolved. And since no one is expected to change their views, there should be no fear of syncretism, the merging of different religious or spiritual traditions. Instead, when we approach interfaith engagement with openness and humility, we arrive at a point where we can admire aspects of other traditions without wanting those aspects for ourselves.[19]

As well as reflecting on the distinctiveness of other faiths and spiritualities, interfaith engagement has made me reflect on my own faith. It wasn't until I started learning about the nuances of other religious or spiritual traditions that I started thinking about the uniqueness and beauty of my own Christian faith. Some believe that spending time with people of other faiths will cause their own faith to suffer.[20] However, I have found that my faith has been nurtured, as I see parts of God's character in the relationships that I build with others and understand more what it means to live faithfully in a multi-faith world. In interfaith engagement, nobody is expected to speak on behalf of their entire religion, but instead they share their personal expression of faith. This means that interfaith engagement does not require us to be entirely secure in our faith but creates an opportunity to grow more confident in our faith and Christian identity.

Building bridges and relationships

As humans, we tend to surround ourselves with similarity. When we do so, we 'lose the capacity to live well with those who are different'.[21] There is a difference between living side by side with people of different faith and spiritual backgrounds and living in interconnected communities. Though all interfaith engagement contributes to the building of a better world, there is benefit in building long-term bridges and relationships. In doing so, we reach out across divisive barriers and learn to live well with our neighbours.[22]

On campus, students can go through their whole university

careers deeply involved in their own faith society, but fail to engage with, or even notice, other faith societies. Interfaith engagement on campus breaks down these boundaries between the different faith societies and brings students together. Spending time with people who are different is potentially risky, since relationships are not predictable and the outcome is unknown. However, if we take a step out of our comfort zone with commitment and vulnerability, the result can be life-changing. It is not just building these multi-faith relationships but modelling them in a way that positively contributes to society. In doing so, we act as witnesses to the possibility and benefit of meaningful relationships between people who appear different.

Building bridges and relationships has value for both the community and the individual involved. Being an extrovert, the chance to meet new people was one of my main motivations for getting involved in interfaith engagement. The friendships I have made are so special because of how they have simultaneously both encouraged and challenged me. Through interfaith engagement, I have found that I often have more in common with those from other faiths or spiritualities than with those of no faith, since we share an experience of practising faith. While at university, I attended a residential for the equipping of interfaith student leaders, run by the Council of Christians and Jews. My fondest memories of the residential are staying up late at night with a Jewish student from a university on the South coast. We spent most of the time laughing, but also sharing with each other our painful experiences of being in halls during our first year at university. Just as I had been supported through that difficult time by my friends at church, so had she been supported by fellow members of her university's Jewish Society.

Interfaith therefore works best when it goes beyond face value encounter. Sajda Majeed (MBE), who has done community work especially with women's interfaith work in Burnley, commented in a recent talk discussing her community's reaction after the Burnley Riots on 22–24 June 2001, we need to move away from cultural awareness and saying, 'Let's have a samosa together, a cup of tea, look at my lovely clothes that I wear' [...] people can think they understand the Asian culture because you've spoken to someone with a headscarf.

Instead, Sajda discusses how it requires long-term commitment, building trust and working together for something that benefits everyone in the community.[23] Sharing food, for instance, opens doors towards understanding but it is not the whole story.

It is important to remember that interfaith engagement is not necessarily neutral ground. Part of building friendships with those of other faiths requires me, as a white Christian, to recognize my privilege. Though good interfaith engagement rests on the principle that we are all equal partners, we must engage with the power dynamics in interfaith friendship that impact the abilities of some partners to trust and participate fully.[24] Growing up as a white Christian in the UK is not the same as growing up in a religious minority. If we are serious about interfaith engagement, we must listen to our friends from religious minorities about their experiences of discrimination and intolerance and stand by them as allies.

Realizing a common humanity

Through interfaith engagement, we discover not just what is distinctive but also what is shared between people of different faiths and spiritualities. I love reflecting on how other people's faith shapes and drives them, in the way that my faith does me. We realize that one of the things that most connect us is the journeying aspect of having a faith; our anxieties, questions and reflections are usually similar, although our practices may be different. Often, what is discovered when bridges and relationships are built is a shared hunger for a better world, and a desire to contribute to its arrival by actively and lovingly engaging in the world.[25]

Final thoughts: interfaith as peace-making

The Beatitudes, part of Jesus' Sermon on the Mount (described in Matthew 5.9), tell us that peace-making is fundamental to what it is to be a Christian and live in the image of God. It is through bringing unity and harmony that we 'act most like God'.[26] Peace-making is not just about avoiding conflict (further explored with Annie Sharples in the next chapter). It is about bringing people together and encouraging them to listen to and learn from each other. Therefore, as well as being a type of social action, interfaith engagement is a method of peace-making that contributes to the reconciling work of God.[27]

In all of this, the Church has a key role to play. There is already some great work happening in the UK, with interfaith programmes being taught in most theological colleges and churches joining local community projects. In Bristol, faith leaders regularly meet on Zoom with representatives from the council to discuss collaboratively how they can best tackle some of the city's social issues, including poverty and racism. However, the Church often views interfaith as an add-on, something that certain individuals are 'called' to. Interfaith must be viewed not in this way but as something that we should all engage in. There is also an ongoing tension associated with evangelism, with some in the Church believing that interfaith engagement provides an opportunity to convert those of other faiths to Christianity. We must move away from viewing people from other religions as targets for evangelism and instead view interfaith engagement as an opportunity to renew our own faith. Leading on this theory, Gaston adopts a 'radical revivalist theology' of interfaith engagement, regarding it as an opportunity for Christian renewal.[28] While at university, I certainly found that interfaith engagement revived my faith, by giving me the confidence and space to express my faith on campus. Though I was regularly attending two (yes, two) churches in Bristol and even studying for a Theology degree, I struggled to talk about my faith with my course-mates and lecturers. I had tried the main evangelical Christian student society but was disappointed by their obsession with traditional types of mission and evangelism. Getting involved in interfaith during my final year gave me a platform for being open about my religious identity on campus, allowing me to talk confidently about my beliefs and practices.

This essay has been a whistle-stop tour of interfaith engagement, from its take-off in the 1960s to where we are now. Though I have focused on my experience of the university campus, interfaith engagement can be done in any context. There are opportunities to interact with people of other faiths and spiritualities in every aspect of life, be it your school, your workplace, at the bus stop or in a coffee shop. And I promise that you will come out the other side of the encounter a better person. In doing so you are joining a movement of people committed to societal transformation, with every interaction contributing to the building of a better world.

Notes

1 E. Patel and P. Brodeur, *Building the Interfaith Youth Movement: Beyond dialogue to action* (Lanham and Oxford: Rowman & Littlefield, 2006).

2 Board for Mission and Unity of the Church of England, *Towards a Theology for Inter-Faith Dialogue* (London: CIO Publishing, 1984), p. 28.

3 S. W. Ariarajah, 'Interfaith Relations within the Emerging Field of World Christianity', in M. Frederiks and D. Nagy (eds), *World Christianity: Methodological Considerations* (Leiden, The Netherlands: Brill, 2020), pp. 135–57, p. 142.

4 I. Ohlen and L. Berndes, 'From Dalaberg to Leicester and back again', in Andrew Wingate and Pernilla Myrelid (eds), *Why Interfaith? Stories, reflections and challenges from recent engagements in Northern Europe* (London: Darton, Longman and Todd, 2016), pp. 198–201, p. 201.

5 R. Boyd, *The Witness of the Student Christian Movement: Church ahead of the Church* (London: SPCK, 2007), pp. 30, 70.

6 Vatican Council, 'Nostra Aetate' (28/08/1965), accessed 29/08/2021 via www.vatican.va/archive/hist_councils/ii_vatican_coun cil/documents/vat-ii_decl_19651028_nostra-aetate_en.html.

7 D. Pratt, Being Open, Being Faithful: The Journey of Interreligious Dialogue (Geneva: WCC Publications, 2014), p. xii.

8 L. Bretherton, 'A Postsecular Politics? Inter-faith Relations as a Civic Practice', in Journal of the American Academy of Religion, 79:2 (2011), pp. 346–377, p. 352.

9 J. Curtice, E. Clery, J. Perry, M. Phillips and N. Rahim (eds), British Social Attitudes: The 36th Report (London: The National Centre for Social Research, 2019), www.bsa.natcen.ac.uk/media/39363/bsa_36. pdf.

10 J. Madeiros, 'Foreword', in R. Sudworth (ed.), Distinctly Welcoming: Christian Presence in a Multifaith Society (Didcot: Scripture Union Publishing, 2007), pp. 14–15.

11 S. Gilliat-Ray, 'Ministerial Formation in a Multi-Faith Society', in Teaching Theology and Religion (6:2, 2002), pp. 9–17, p. 16.

12 UK Government, 'Social Action', accessed 18/04/2021 via www. gov.uk/government/publications/centre-for-social-action/centre-for-social-action

13 Pratt, Being Open, Being Faithful, p. vii.

14 E. Graham, 'Introduction', in R. Gaston, Faith, Hope and Love: Interfaith Engagement as Practical Theology (London: SCM Press, 2017), p. x.

15 G. Jarvis (2016), 'Neighbours', in Wingate and Myrelid (eds), Why Interfaith? pp. 10–15, p. 13.

16 Ibid.

17 Sudworth, Distinctly Welcoming, p. 90.

18 I. Maher, 'Sheffield Hallam University', in M. Threlfall-Holmes and M. Newitt (eds), Being a Chaplain (London: SPCK, 2011), pp. 27–9.

19 B. Brown Taylor, Holy Envy: Finding God in the Faith of Others (New York: HarperCollins Publishers, 2018).

20 T. Wilson, Hospitality, Service, Proclamation: Interfaith Engagement as Christian Discipleship (London: SCM Press, 2014).

21 R. Ravat and T. Wilson, Learning to Live Well Together: Case Studies in Interfaith Diversity (London: Jessica Kingsley Publishers, 2017), p. 32.

22 Wingate and Myrelid eds., Why Interfaith, p. xv.

23 S. Majeed, 'Burnley Riots', Talk for the Journey of Hope Pilgrimage 2021 (26/03/2021) https://stethelburgas.org/projects/reconcilerstogether/.

24 Ravat and Wilson, Learning to Live Well Together, p. 108.

25 See M. Duncan, *Building a Better World: Faith at Work for Change in Society* (London: Continuum, 2006), p. 66; Jarvis, 'Neighbours', p. 10.

26 Duncan, *Building a Better World*, p. 70.

27 Jarvis, 'Neighbours', p. 15.

28 Gaston, *Faith, Hope and Love*, p. 82.

13

Our Call to Real Peace

ANNIE SHARPLES

Introduction

Peace is huge. Peace is crucial, not only for the world but for every individual. World peace and the end of all wars and conflicts are absolutely necessary. The way I view peace, however, and the way I think it is most helpful and useful, is that peace is more than the absence of conflict. Peace encapsulates all aspects of society and each living thing. To seek peace and reconciliation is the responsibility of every person.

Shalom is a Hebrew word often translated as 'peace'. In her book on violence in the Old Testament, Helen Paynter uses a much more all-encompassing definition of Shalom which I think is valuable:

Although loosely translated 'peace', it actually encapsulates a much more holistic vision than that. Perhaps an analogy would be helpful. Think for a moment of how you would define the word 'health'. In 1946, the World Health Organisation defined it like this: 'Health is a state of complete physical, mental and social well-being and not merely the absence of disease of infirmity'.[1] This beautiful, holistic definition of health – which cannot be said of someone who is the subject of domestic violence, or suffers chronic anxiety, or lives in grinding poverty – is rather similar to the biblical concept of shalom. The word 'shalom', as used in the Bible, has a wide semantic range – in other words, it has a wide scatter of related meanings. The core meaning relates to completeness or intactness, and the range of meanings includes prosperity, welfare, good relationships, deliverance and health.[2]

A member of the Iona Community used 'Shalom/Salaam', using both the Hebraic and Arabic translations of peace in the same breath, embodying reconciliation in the words he intentionally used – bringing together the Jewish and Islamic traditions, joining these words together immediately demonstrates a core reconciliation aim of peace across the Jewish/Muslim divide. Shalom/Salaam.

Peace, to me, would be all things in harmony, all things equal, right and just, where everyone and everything on the planet are living together, safe, content and able to reach their full potential. Peace is not simply the absence of war and conflict, though you cannot have *full peace* while wars and conflicts rage.

My sister is a big fan of the enneagram, a model of nine personality types, interconnected, yet each with their own core desires and fears. The model is often used within teams to help members understand each other. I am a type nine, the mediator or the peacemaker. My basic desire in all situations is to have wholeness and peace. My basic fear is conflict, loss and separation. Avoiding conflicts is almost instinctual for me. Which is problematic! My sister often laughs at me, saying 'You're just such a nine', meaning that I shy away from conflict in an attempt to keep 'peace'. Supressing conflict, however, is not peace. Peace does not come from ignoring conflict, peace comes from reconciling conflicts. Peace is the ideal and the aim we are striving for. Reconciliation is the process by which we get there. Reconciliation is the hard, often painful and raw journey that involves turning back toward the conflict, facing it and dealing with it, not so that it can be forgotten, but in order to move on and find peace in what had happened.

I find it useful to break peace down into three interconnected levels: personal, social and political. Personal peace is having peace within our own selves, being aware of, and in tune with, our feelings and reactions. Social peace is living peaceably with those around us, those we come into contact with daily; social peace is more about relationships and community. Finally, political peace is the widest level, working towards peace in society, nations, systems and structures. Shalom/salaam can be applied to each of these levels, but for true shalom/salaam, there has to be peace at all levels for all beings.

Personal peace

Personal peace is about being at peace with ourselves, reconciled with who we are. The ease or difficulty of this varies with each individual and their circumstances, but finding peace within ourselves is important for our mental well-being. This 'inner peace' is associated with spiritual and mindfulness practices such as yoga and meditation. If each of the three levels of peace work together and feed into each other, then inner peace, this personal peace of any individual, contributes to wider and greater peace, right through to world peace. In the Buddhist tradition, long associated with peace and non-violence, there is a belief that all things, however small or large, however far apart, are inextricably and fundamentally related, and that distinctions made between individuals and the universe are misleading and untrue.[3] The Dalai Lama says:

> The question of real, lasting world peace concerns human beings, so basic human feelings are also at its roots. Through inner peace, genuine world peace can be achieved. In this the importance of individual responsibility is quite clear; an atmosphere of peace must first be created within ourselves, then gradually expanded to include our families, our communities, and ultimately the whole planet.[4]

Any type of peace, however small, contributes to the wider effort for peace and a complete shalom/salaam. We all can be, and are, peacemakers.

John Paul Lederach, known for his work in conflict transformation and reconciliation, talks about inward compassion. Compassion is generally seen as something that is projected outward, given to others, which, Lederach argues, makes compassion an act of superiority and creates a power dynamic between those outside the difficult situation and those who are suffering.[5] He maintains that we rarely provide ourselves with compassion; 'we don't conceive of the notion that our inner self requires patience, accompaniment, care and reflection on the fullness of who we are – light and shadow included'.[6] He goes on to argue that 'self-care and reflection must not be understood as instruments for the real work. They *are* the work of reconciliation'.[7]

Social peace

The next level in our three levels of peace is social peace. This is primarily about relationships and living peaceably with and in our communities and social groups. The key is listening, understanding and empathizing. Peace does not mean the absence of disagreement. Conflict is a natural and necessary part of life and relationships. Peace comes in how we react, respond and live with disagreements. Living in community and being in relationship with others is so much harder, arguably impossible, without reconciliation.

I spent three years of my childhood living on the Isle of Iona in Scotland, as part of the Iona Community, in residential community. As a child I was blissfully unaware of the often difficult nature of living in intentional community with others. I now realize how much energy, time and understanding the residents had to give in order to maintain good relationships and remain a community.

Much of reconciliation is about being alongside others. It requires openness to see and welcome the humanity in the other, as Lederach puts it, 'to feel the world from their perspective, and to place ourselves not in control of but *alongside* the human experience and condition'.[8] This notion of being 'alongside' is crucial. Jesus is a really good example of someone who did this frequently, well, and with those who were avoided or ignored. The gospels are full of occurrences of Jesus meeting, listening to and eating with those in the lowest echelons of society: the sick, the poor, the cast out. Jesus often eats with people, and this is an instance in which both parties are on the same level. They are eating the same food, sat together and sharing at the same table. Lederach again:

> Across almost all cultures, eating together implies relationship and connection. In the international area we use tables as a metaphor for coming together to talk, negotiate, and seek peace. Eating symbolizes a universal truth that we are connected in the broader human race ... Eating together puts us on the same level. When we are working in complicated international negotiations, eating together often provides a different way for people to connect with and see each other. When we eat together, we are on the same social place, we admit our sameness, and we recognize our basic humanity. In this sense, eating is a safe space, a place where we are ourselves.[9]

I would also argue that walking together does a similar and equally powerful thing. I am a big fan of pilgrimage. In 2019, walking from Bristol to Tolpuddle, a co-pilgrim shared that in walking side-by-side with another it is easier to talk, be open and be together because you are physically travelling together, you are looking at the same view, the same surroundings, you share the commonality of that specific journey, and also, in walking alongside another, the sometimes confrontational feeling of being face-to-face is removed, you are next to rather than opposite one another. If you take this as a metaphor for reconciliation, then you return to the notion of getting alongside the other. It is easier to recognize the humanity in others when you are doing something together, be that eating or walking.

At the Greenbelt Festival in 2018, I was moved by hearing Jo Berry in conversation with Pat Magee. Jo's father was killed in the IRA Brighton bombing in 1984. Pat Magee was the man who planted that bomb. Jo talked about her desire to simply understand Pat's actions so they met together in 2000. For Jo, 'it was all about humanizing the other ... I don't want to blame him,' she said, 'I just want to listen and understand and hear his story.' When they met, they talked together for three hours, and Jo said 'I've looked into Pat's eyes and I've seen he cares, I've seen his humanity ... I can experience him as a human being, beyond what he did'. It is this recognition of the other as a fellow human that is crucial. 'It isn't even about forgiving, it's about empathy and understanding', Jo said.[10] Jo and Pat have travelled and toured together, sharing their story, working for peace and promoting reconciliation. They call one another friends.

When I re-listened to this talk, I was struck by the image of them shaking hands when they met. A handshake is a widespread action between two people that is often shared in greeting, and is said to originate as a gesture conveying peaceful intentions, revealing an outstretched, empty hand, thus demonstrating a lack of weapons. If you delve deeper into the gesture, you can see symbols of openness, welcome, generosity, togetherness. A connection is made between two people after the physical touch of hands, an undeniable recognition of one another's humanity.

Pádraig Ó Tuama's poem 'Shaking Hands' explores this notion further. The poem was written in response to Martin McGuinness, the Deputy First Minister of the Northern Ireland Assembly, and Queen Elizabeth II shaking hands for the first time, following The Troubles in Northern Ireland in the twentieth century, which was a hugely significant gesture.[11]

Shaking Hands
27ú lá Meitheamh, 2012

Because what's the alternative?
Because of courage.
Because of loved ones lost.
Because no more.
Because it's a small thing; shaking hands; it happens
   every day.
Because I heard of one man whose hands haven't stopped
   shaking since a market day in Omagh.
Because it takes a second to say hate, but it takes longer,
   much longer, to be a great leader.
Much, much longer.
Because shared space without human touching doesn't
   amount to much.
Because it's easier to speak to your own than to hold
   the hand of someone whose side has been previously
   described, proscribed, denied.
Because it is tough.
Because it is tough.
Because it is meant to be tough, and this is the stuff of
   memory, the stuff of hope, the stuff of gesture, and
   meaning and leading.
Because it has taken so, so long.
Because it has taken land and money and languages and
   barrels and barrels of blood and grieving.
Because lives have been lost.
Because lives have been taken.
Because to be bereaved is to be troubled by grief.
Because more than two troubled peoples live here.
Because I know a woman whose hand hasn't been shaken
   since she was a man.
Because shaking a hand is only a part of the start.
Because I know a woman whose touch calmed a man whose
   heart was breaking.
Because privilege is not to be taken lightly.

Because this just might be good.
Because who said that this would be easy?
Because some people love what you stand for, and for some,
    if you can, they can.
Because solidarity means a common hand.
Because a hand is only a hand; so hang onto it.
So join your much discussed hands.
We need this; for one small second.
So touch.
So lead.

(© Pádraig Ó Tuama 2012)

Political peace

The final level of peace is the one most associated with the word peace, and that is political peace, which is peace between and in nations, the end of wars and full disarmament. If we return to our definition of shalom/salaam, political peace also includes equality, where all can prosper, have enough to eat and resources are shared based on need rather than wealth. Wars and conflicts will continue to rage while there continues to be injustices like the climate crisis/the use of fossil fuels, gender inequality, racism, poverty, economic injustice, religious intolerance, and more. All inequalities and injustices negate peace. A global shalom/salaam would mean that all nations and the global population of all creatures and living things are able to coexist in harmony, where all things are good, equal and just.

According to the International Campaign Against Nuclear Weapons (ICAN), there are more than 13,400 nuclear weapons in current arsenals, nine nuclear armed states and 32 states that endorse nuclear weapons.[12] In their Enough is Enough report on the global spending on nuclear weapons in 2019, ICAN estimated that the nine nuclear armed states spent $72.9 billion on their nuclear weapons, which equates to $138,699 spent every minute of 2019.[13]

As I write, the British Government has confirmed plans to increase the cap and relax restrictions on nuclear weapons, with plans to extend the UK's nuclear stockpile by 40 per cent, from 180 warheads to 260.[14] This marks the end of the UK's gradual disarmament over the last 30 years, since the end of the Soviet Union. The plans are actually illegal, as increasing the UK's nuclear stockpile breaks the Non-Proliferation Treaty that Britain ratified in 1970.[15] These proposals followed an announcement cutting the UK's foreign aid budget on the grounds of unaffordability, showing that the UK is prioritizing unnecessary weapons of mass destruction over sending aid and support to people and places already torn apart by conflict and poverty. Rather than help in a small way to get slightly closer to a state of shalom/salaam, these plans take us a long way in the opposite direction.

A peace activist recalls being on pilgrimage from Iona to London to deliver a petition against nuclear weapons. When they passed through Glasgow, they met young people unaware that the Trident base was so close to where they lived. When they discovered this, they were quick to sign the petition and ask what else they could do. Isaiah 2.4 depicts a hopeful vision of the community of God:

He shall judge between the nations,
    and shall arbitrate for many peoples;
they shall beat their swords into ploughshares,
    and their spears into pruning hooks;
nation shall not lift up sword against nation,
    neither shall they learn war any more.
(Isaiah 2.4, NRSV)

This imagines all conflicts being reconciled and all weapons being transformed into tools for growing and harvesting food and tending to the land, rather than used for violence and destruction. An action that really brings this vision to life is the planting of flowers by Iona Community members near the gates of Faslane, where Trident, the UK's nuclear weapons, are based. Now, on passing the gates of Faslane, people see signs of hope, beauty and life. I believe this is our calling as Christians and as humans: to sow seeds of hope, whether literal or metaphorical, and to work for peace and justice, campaigning, striving and waiting for the day when a global shalom/salaam is achieved.

These are just a few examples of the activism of older members of the Iona Community. Since my early childhood, these individuals and their action in their commitment to justice and peace, based on their faith, have inspired me and made me realize that this is what the whole Church should be doing. This was what Church was, is, about. The legacy of these tireless individuals is what brings me hope for what the Church could be.

Methodism began in the eighteenth century, founded on social justice. The first Methodist building, the New Room in Bristol, where I worked recently, was built in 1739 as a community centre. Throughout the week there was food and clothing for those unable to afford it, education, free medical care and collections for prisoners, social peace etc. With such a rich history of working for justice, why is it no longer obviously evident in so much of Methodism today? Justice and peace must be priorities for all denominations. Deeply influenced and shaped by Methodism, I feel strongly that this must return to the heart of our Church, in teaching and in action.

In 2020, faith leaders signed a letter against nuclear weapons, urging the UK Government to sign the UN Treaty, a powerful and unifying statement.[16] But this is not good enough. It is comparable to institutions declaring a climate emergency and then continuing business as usual in an unsustainable way, without making any significant changes. Churches, religious leaders and people of faith need to be campaigning actively against nuclear weapons.

Conclusion

I am currently volunteering with the Iona Community. As part of the daily morning worship, we say in the closing responses, 'we will seek peace and pursue it' (Psalm 34). I really appreciate being challenged every morning to renew my commitment to peace and reconciliation. Hearing others say these words with me reaffirms this even more. The prayers also include the responses 'Love and faith come together, justice and peace join hands' (Psalm 85:10). This stirs up an image of these four critical beings, if you will, coming together, holding hands and enabling the vision in Isaiah 2. Any one of these four are almost redundant without the other three; there is no justice without peace, faith is redundant without love, peace must include all kinds of love. Similarly, part of the Rule of the Iona Community, is *Working for justice and peace, wholeness and reconciliation in our localities, society and the whole creation*, and again, any one of these four are impossible without the others. By including 'wholeness' with justice, peace and reconciliation, it is acknowledging the notion of wholeness binding us together so that our actions for peace are integrated into a holistic commitment to the well-being of all. All four of both of these sets are relevant and desperately needed for all three of our levels of peace.

In *Peacework*, Henri Nouwen argues that fear is the biggest threat to peace.[17] Fear manifests in different ways for different people and different situations, including pride, greed, selfishness, resistance to change, etc. Commonly, fear of the other and fear of what is different causes so much conflict. Perhaps because we feel scared about being dominated or forced to change. Churches should be places and communities where the emphasis is on overcoming this fear, bringing different people and views together, not to assimilate but to understand. So much of the Iona Community youth programme was incredibly formative and important for me, through bringing together young people who otherwise would never have met. People who, on the surface, had so little in common, but when you spent a week in community, or a weekend learning together, found that assumptions were broken down. There would be young people from deprived, inner-city areas, from wealthy, privileged families, refugees, wealthy Americans, and we were all brought together and learnt so much in such a rich and powerful way. So much of what prevents peace stems from some sort of fear. We need to recognize this, step back and look at how fear is playing its part in our lives, our relationships with others, our way of seeing ourselves, others and the world. When we are able to address and resolve this, we are able to begin reconciliation of self, of society and of the world of politics, which is the journey towards peace.

Blessed are the peacemakers.

Notes

1 World Health Organisation, www.who.int/about/who-we-are/constitution.

2 H. Paynter, *God of Violence Yesterday, God of Love Today? Wrestling Honestly with the Old Testament* (Abingdon: Bible Reading Fellowship, 2019), pp. 156–7.

3 K. Kraft (ed.), *Inner Peace, World Peace: Essays on Buddhism and Nonviolence* (Albany: State University of New York Press, 1992), p. 2.

4 T. Gyatso, '14th Dalai Lama', as quoted in K. Kraft, *Inner Peace*, p. 2.

5 J. P. Lederach, *Reconcile: Conflict Transformation for Ordinary Christians* (Harrisonburg, VA: Herald Press, 2014), p. 51.

6 Ibid.

7 Lederach, *Reconcile*, p. 54.

8 Lederach, *Reconcile*, p. 56.

9 Lederach, *Reconcile*, pp. 106–7.

10 J. Berry and P. Magee, 'Beyond Forgiveness: The Supreme Act of Imagination', *Greenbelt 2018*, accessed 28/05/2021 via, www.greenbelt.org.uk/talks/beyond-forgiveness-the-supreme-act-of-imagination/

11 Pádraig Ó Tuama, *Sorry For Your Troubles* (Norwich: Canterbury Press, 2013), p. 79.

12 International Campaign Against Nuclear Weapons, accessed 28/05/2015, via www.icanw.org/

13 ICAN, *Enough is Enough: 2019 Global Nuclear Weapons*

Spending, accessed 22/08/2021 via https://d3n8a8pro7vhmx.cloud front.net/ican/pages/1549/attachments/original/1589365383/ ICAN-Enough-is-Enough-Global-Nuclear-Weapons-Spending-2020-published-13052020.pdf?1589365383, p. 3.

14 D. Sabbagh, 'Cap on Trident nuclear warhead stockpile to rise by more than 40%', accessed 28/05/2021 via www.theguardian.com/uk-news/2021/mar/15/cap-on-trident-nuclear-warhead-stockpile-to-rise-by-more-than-40

15 Campaign for Nuclear Disarmament, 'No more Nukes: Time to Scrap Trident', accessed 27/05/2021 via https://cnduk.org/no-more-nukes-time-to-scrap-trident/

16 Churches Together in Britain and Ireland, 'Church leaders oppose expansion of nuclear weapons', accessed 20/05/2021 via https://ctbi.org.uk/church-leaders-oppose-expansion-of-nuclear-weapons/

17 H. Nouwen, *Peacework* (Maryknoll, NY: Orbis Books, 2015), p. 35.

Contributors

Anthony G. Reddie

Anthony is the Director of the Oxford Centre for Religion and Culture and an A-rated Leading International Researcher with the South African National Research Foundation (NRF). He is also a recipient of the Archbishop of Canterbury's 2020 Lanfranc Award for 'exceptional and sustained contribution to Black theology in Britain and beyond'. His recent books are *Theologising Brexit: A Liberationist and Postcolonial Critique* (Routledge, 2019), and the republished *Is God Colour Blind? Insights from Black Theology for Christian faith and Ministry* (SPCK, 2020) and *Intercultural Preaching* (co-edited with Seidel Abel Boargenes and Pamela Searle; Regent's Park College, 2021).

Samuel Nwokoro

Sam Nwokoro is a student of history. He was born in the city of Jos, Nigeria. Sam identifies with the Anglican community in Edinburgh, where he currently lives. In his spare time, he enjoys writing, running and swing dancing.

Victoria Turner

Victoria is currently a PhD Candidate in World Christianity at the University of Edinburgh, exploring the mission of the Iona

Community and the Council for World Mission. Her studies are sponsored by the Council for World Mission's Special Academic Accompaniment Programme. She is a member of the United Reformed Church and sits on the URC-Baptist Union Interfaith Enabling Group. Victoria is also a Trustee for Churches Together in England and the Society for Ecumenical Studies, a Tearfund Young Theologian, and the editor of the Student Christian Movement's *Movement* magazine. She has recently started a Palestinian Liberation Theology Reading Group.

Liz Marsh

Liz graduated from the University of Edinburgh with an MA(Hons) in Theology and completed a Masters at Vrije Universiteit Amsterdam before spending two years as a lay pastoral assistant in a Nottingham parish. She has recently returned to Edinburgh to pursue a PhD in the theology of hope in the context of ecological crisis. Liz has been involved in the Student Christian Movement since 2014 and is currently an Associate Editor for *Macrina* magazine.

Nosayaba Idehen

Nosa is a Biochemistry graduate from the University of Lancaster. After her degree she became one of three London Baptist Association interns and has subsequently been appointed a Charity Trustee for the London Baptist Association. Nosa is currently a medical student.

Josh Mock

Josh Mock is a BA Arabic and Persian student at SOAS, University of London. A lifelong Anglican, he has been active in the Student Christian Movement of Great Britain and has sat on the board of trustees. Josh's research interests include queer theologies, Middle Eastern and Islamic studies, and international relations. A graduate of the Purcell School for Young Musicians, Josh is also a cellist and composer. Josh loves baking, particularly sourdough bread, and having interesting conversations over coffee.

Molly Boot

Molly is 24 and is a theologian, broadcaster and musician. Her academic work focuses on power, medieval mysticism, sacramentality and the arts, and she has also written on trauma theology, queer theology and theologies of consent. Molly is a Church of England ordinand at St Augustine's College and St Matthew's Church, Bethnal Green. She is a trustee of the Greenbelt Festival, and when she isn't writing, she can usually be found playing the violin, conducting or preaching.

Kirsty Bothwick

Kirsty is serving as deacon and Assistant Curate at All Saints Church, Leighton Buzzard in the Diocese of St Albans. She is currently completing her PhD at the University of Cambridge and spent a year at the World Council of Churches Bossey Institute learning about World Christianity and Ecumenism.

Laura Cook

Laura works as a Communications Advisor with The Elders, an organization founded by Nelson Mandela in 2007. The Elders are independent global leaders working together for peace and human rights. Her background is in humanitarian aid and international development with a particular interest and experience in forced migration studies. She is also on the steering group of EP2030, an ecumenical Christian movement, an expression of the Micah Global Network formed to engage, equip and empower the Church to take action on the Sustainable Development Goals. She is a professional humanitarian photographer and writer and a spoken word poet.

Jack Woodruff

Jack is a mathematician and Christian working for LGBTQ+ rights, peace and the climate. In 2020 he graduated from the University of York with a Masters in Mathematics. He has been involved with a variety of organizations committed to putting faith into action, including the Student Christian Movement, the Fellowship of Reconciliation, FaithJustice UK and currently as a volunteer on Iona with the Iona Community.

Chrissie Thwaites

Chrissie's current research focuses on purity culture in contemporary Christianity, and the impact this has had within UK evangelicalism. She joined the University of Leeds in October 2020 as a PhD student, funded by an AHRC White Rose College of the Arts and Humanities (WRoCAH) scholarship. Prior to this, she completed BA and MA degrees at the University of Exeter. She is a Tearfund Young Theologian and her Masters thesis explored disability justice in UK churches.

Anna Twomlow

Anna currently works for the World Resource Institute researching behavioural science and climate change. She has previously worked for the World Food Program researching food systems, and Imperial College London researching natural disasters and humanitarian crises. She was raised in Zimbabwe, went to high school in Kenya and has worked in the UK, Spain and Italy. She considers herself a true 'Third Culture Kid'. She is passionate about justice and equality, for people and Mother Nature. Anna is a seventh-generation Methodist, and her family lore suggests that her great, great, great, great, great, great grandparents met John Wesley! She currently attends Hinde Street Methodist Church in London, where she regularly asks uncomfortable questions, and was a member of the Community of St Anselm in 2019–2020, where her passion for ecumenism was ignited.

Annika Mathews

Annika is currently based in south-east England but has lived across England and in Romania. She has experience of copyediting, interning with churches, a school chaplaincy charity and teaching English abroad. Her studies were in Classics and Archaeology. She loves animals, walking, singing, baking, travelling and seeing friends and family. She is passionate about the climate, God and social justice issues of all kinds. Annika is a trustee of a youth work charity and has been involved in a variety of local and national church groups including the Churches Together in England Enabling Group, General Synod and the Church of England Anti-Racism Task-force group. She is ecumenical at heart and has worshipped in a variety of churches. She hopes to study theology and become a priest at some point!

Shermara Fletcher

Shermara is serving as the Principal Officer for Pentecostal, Charismatic and Multi-cultural Relations at Churches Together in England. With roots in the Church of God of Prophecy, Shermara is a dynamic millennial Pentecostal leader with significant experience in community organizing, ecumenical engagement, leadership development and public speaking. Shermara recently contributed a chapter to the book *Coming Home: Christian perspectives on housing*, edited by Graham Tomlin and Canon Malcolm Brown. In recognition of her ground-breaking work, Shermara was the recipient of the 2020 Exceptional Young Woman award from The Wise Women Awards.

Sophie Mitchell

After graduating with a Theology and Sociology BA at the University of Bristol in 2019, Sophie became the Chaplaincy Assistant at the University's Multifaith Chaplaincy. Interfaith engagement was a key part of life for Sophie during university, as a member of the University's Student Multifaith Forum and a campus leader for the Council of Christians and Jews. She was also a youth representative on the General Synod of the Church of England. Currently, Sophie is fulfilling her postponed travelling dreams.

Annie Sharples

Annie is a Methodist and has been involved with the Iona Community since childhood, and is currently volunteering on Iona. Annie is part of both the Young Adults' Group and the Peace, Reconciliation and Disarmament Common Concern Network of the Iona Community. She graduated from the University of Kent with a degree in History and English Literature, and did a year's internship at the New Room/John Wesley's Chapel in Bristol, which is the oldest Methodist building in the world. During her internship, she carried out an oral history project and curated an exhibition telling the more recent and personal history of the New Room.